THE SIN DECEPTION

Exposing The Lies That Bind

By

Walter Leathers

Published by Book Writing Genie
Cover design by Book Writing Genie
ISBN: Printed in the United States

Table of Contents

Dedication

To God, the Father, Jesus, my Lord and Savior, and the Holy Spirit, my constant Companion and Comforter, This book is humbly dedicated to your glory.

To my fellow humanity struggling in a fallen world ruled by the kingdom of sin,

May this book offer guidance, encouragement, and the promise of victory through Jesus Christ.

To those battling sin's grip,

Don't lose heart! Keep struggling, stay in the fight. Your victory is assured through faith in Jesus. You are not alone.

With love and gratitude, I dedicate this book to:

My family, dear to my heart,

I love you more than words can express.

Joel and Jean Gay, faithful friends and burden-bearers,

Thank you for enriching my life with love, grace, and unwavering support.

Tim, my brother

Your stable voice and constant companionship have been a lifeline. You and Rhonda are amazing friends to journey life with.

To my dear friends Michael (MJ to me) and Becky, thank you for sharing your time and encouraging my efforts.

With special affection for my friend and a first-class ambassador for the kingdom of God, Shirley Jungbuth. I am forever grateful for the prayers.

Finally, I would also like to thank Lee Strobel, Be Bold, for the Jesus conference. Wow, what a blessing. Keep pushing the Kingdom forward!

May this book honor God and inspire hope in the hearts of all who read it.

Acknowledgment

I am deeply grateful to the many individuals who have supported and encouraged me throughout the writing of 'The Sin Deception: Exposing the Lies that Bind.'

To my friends and family, your unwavering belief in me and this project has meant the world. I am blessed to have two loving parents, and I am grateful they gave me a place to stay when I needed it most. Your prayers, listening ears, and words of encouragement have sustained me through the darkest of times.

Special thanks to Maria Estrada, who was the first to offer feedback, suggestions, and encouragement. Your input was invaluable, and your enthusiasm helped spark the flame that kept me going.

I also want to extend a special thank you to the Wednesday night group at Harvest Assembly in Rosalia, WA. The food, fellowship, and fun we shared each week were a highlight of my journey. Preparing for the weekly message was both difficult and challenging, but it also led to a deeper knowledge and faith. I am grateful to each of you for becoming like family to me, and I will always thank God for the blessings that came from being part of this group.

I remain convinced that the message of this book is crucial for our times.

Thank you again to each and everyone who has played a part in bringing this book to life. May God bless you richly for your support and encouragement.

About the Author

As a fellow traveler, I'm honored to share my reflections with you. I am so grateful to God, whose transformative love and sacrifice have shaped my path and inspired my writing.

A veteran of the US Navy and US Army, I've been blessed with diverse experiences, including a 20-year career in vocational education, focusing on skills and knowledge people actually use. My travels across the country have broadened my perspectives about life, people and the world, but it's my 35 years of studying the Bible under the Holy Spirit's guidance that has deepened my understanding and convinced me to write.

I've been blessed to participate in lots of Bible studies, and I have had the chance to share God's Word many times, including through social media. I have been blessed to be able to participate in service by providing food and Bibles where we could.

My heart's desire is to teach relationship over religion, encouraging daily time in the Word and prayer.

Through my experiences, God has taught me the importance of exposing the lies that bind us and revealing the truth about sin. This passion led me to write "The Sin Deception." I pray that this book will help others break free from deception and find freedom in Christ.

I'm not perfect, and my journey is ongoing. But I'm grateful for God's patience and guidance. My goal is to point others to Jesus, not to myself. I pray that my story and teachings will inspire others to seek a deeper relationship with God.

Author's Note

Ladies and gentlemen of America. I've noticed that you're extremely interested in spiritual things. Your cities are filled with idols, and you even have an altar dedicated to the unknown God. This tells me that you're aware of a higher power, but you're not quite sure who He is or how to connect with Him.

You've created idols to represent God, but these idols are just mere representations of your own imagination. The true God is the Creator of the universe, the One who gives life and breath to all things. He doesn't need our temples or sacrifices; instead, He wants us to seek Him and worship Him in spirit and truth.

You think you can find fulfillment and meaning in life through your own efforts, but the truth is, we're all dependent on God. He's the One who gives us life, breath, and everything we need. Our existence is not about us; it's about Him.

You believe that God is only concerned with certain people or groups, but the truth is that He's the God of all nations, and His message is for everyone. He wants all people to repent and turn to Him.

Paul's message to the Athenians is just as relevant today. We still struggle with idolatry, self-sufficiency, and exclusion. But the truth remains: God is the Creator, Sustainer, and Redeemer of all. Yes, beloved, those are the words of Paul to the people in Athens with a modern update. It still applies, don't you think?

Preface

The Sin Deception: The Lies That Bind was born out of my personal journey and passion to uncover the complexities of sin.

For years, I've walked alongside individuals trapped in addiction, witnessing the frustrating cycle of behavior modification and 12-step programs. I've seen how distorted views of sin can leave people feeling helpless.

As I delved deeper, I realized we've been misled about sin's true nature. Half-truths and ineffective strategies have left us vulnerable. Society's redefined language obscures truth, making it challenging to grasp. Our limited understanding of sin serves a sinister purpose: keeping us enslaved.

I've come to see sin's vast reach and the depths of human depravity. Its tenacious grip destroys lives, relationships, and communities. We've been sold a watered-down version of sin, reducing it to mere mistakes or weaknesses. But sin is more insidious. It's a master manipulator, disguising itself as harmless desires or cultural norms.

The consequences of this deception are staggering. We're left struggling with addiction, brokenness, and shame. Our incomplete understanding of sin hinders true freedom. Through my journey, I've uncovered the complexity of sin, including its destructive power, subtle deceit, and ability to masquerade as harmless or even good.

This understanding has also led me to explore the biblical perspective on sin. I've discovered that sin is a choice, not just a condition, with its origins in human rebellion. I've seen God's plan to redeem and restore, and the transformative power of Jesus Christ.

This realization ignites a sense of urgency within me. We must confront sin's deception and seek truth. Only then can we break free from its grip and find redemption. In "The Sin Deception," I share my findings, exploring sin's nuances and the path to liberation. Join me on this journey toward understanding and freedom.

Through my research and experiences, I've gained insight into the nuances of sin as a noun, verb, and kingdom. I've explored the origin of sin, its staggering cost, and God's progressive revelation of the sacrificial system, culminating in Jesus, the Lamb of God. This book clarifies the distinctions between sin, evil, and the devil, shedding light on breaking free from the kingdom of sin and entering the Kingdom of God.

Writing this book has come at a great personal cost. Amidst the turmoil of divorce, financial ruin, and lost relationships, I've clung to my faith, knowing Jesus is my Lord and Savior. Why persevere? Because sin is a universal issue affecting us all. Jesus emphasized sin's significance, speaking about it more than any other topic.

I invite you to study this book, not just read it. Explore the Scriptures, and let God's Word ignite faith within you. Understanding sin is crucial, but it's only the beginning. Together, let's confront sin and find freedom in the truth.

1 John 2:1 – "My dear children, I write this to you so that you will not sin. But if anybody does sin, we have an advocate with the Father—Jesus Christ, the Righteous One.

Chapter 1
The Great Deception

"Humanity is born with a bent towards sin, bearing its weight from the start."

– R.C. Sproul

For centuries, humanity has grappled with the complexities of sin, yet the truth remains intentionally shrouded in mystery. Incomplete information and deliberate lies have distorted our understanding, perpetuating a cycle of confusion and oppression.

Organized religions and nation-states have intentionally concealed the truth, exploiting the ambiguity for power and financial gain. By manipulating the narrative, they have enthroned the kingdom of sin, dictating what is right and wrong.

The consequences are far-reaching. People have been subjugated, marginalized and silenced. Institutions have amassed wealth and influence, solidifying their grip on power.

This deception has tainted our perception of morality, fostering a culture of fear and guilt. We've been conditioned to conform rather than question the status quo.

The time has come to expose the truth. To unravel the tangled threads of misinformation and uncover the authentic meaning of sin.

Do I really believe there is an intentional plan to prevent people from knowing the whole truth? Do I honestly think that there is organized opposition to a complete understanding of sin? Am I trying to tell you that the church keeps you in the dark for power and control?

Absolutely!

Let me illustrate how far the church has gone to prevent you from knowing the truth.

William Tyndale, a hero of faith and a pivotal figure in Christian history, dared to challenge the established order of the church in the 16th century.

Born around 1494 in Melksham Court, Stinchcombe, Gloucestershire, England, Tyndale was driven by an unwavering passion to make the Bible accessible to the masses. His quest for biblical truth and linguistic expertise led him to become one of the earliest translators of the Bible into English.

Seems like a kind and generous thing to do. Imagine being turned into a criminal for simply sharing the truth in plain English.

Tyndale's journey began during his studies at Oxford University, where he became enamored with the ideas of the Renaissance humanists and the reformers. He was particularly drawn to the teachings of Erasmus, who advocated for a return to the original Greek and Hebrew texts of Scripture. This exposure ignited a fire within Tyndale, compelling him to dedicate his life to translating the Bible into the vernacular language of the common people. However, this endeavor was considered radical and threatening by the church, which sought to maintain control over the interpretation and dissemination of Scripture.

Of course, they did; beloved, control is power.

The Church's opposition stemmed from its desire to preserve its authority and maintain the status quo. By keeping the Bible in Latin, a language only accessible to the educated elite, the clergy could dictate the narrative and ensure that the laity remained dependent on them for spiritual guidance. Tyndale's translation would have empowered the common man to engage directly with Scripture, undermining the Church's grip on power. The clergy feared that widespread biblical literacy would lead directly to a personal relationship with God and, ultimately, the erosion of their authority.

Despite the risks, Tyndale persevered, relying on patrons and sympathetic supporters to fund his work. In 1526, he published his New Testament translation in Worms, Germany, which was smuggled into England.

The reaction was swift and brutal; the Church condemned Tyndale's work, and King Henry VIII ordered his arrest. After years in hiding, Tyndale was betrayed, captured and executed in Vilvoorde, near Brussels, on October 6, 1536.

Did you catch that? King Henry VIII had him captured and killed. You might be wondering why the King of England ordered Tyndale's execution. What do the church and the state have to do with each other? Shouldn't the Pope order the execution if he is the head of the church and this is a spiritual matter?

Historically, the church and power in the form of kings, empires, powerful rulers and global movements have had love-hate relationships with one another. They use each other, work together and often betray one another in the never-ending quest for power. In medieval Europe, the Catholic Church held immense power and influence, shaping laws, culture and politics. The state, in turn, supported the church, enforcing its doctrines and authority.

The church and the state conspire to keep power and control.

During the Middle Ages, the church and state cooperated closely. The church legitimized monarchs, and in return, rulers protected church interests. This symbiotic relationship benefited both parties, solidifying their power. However, this cooperation often led to oppression, as dissenting voices were silenced and minority groups faced persecution.

As the Renaissance and Reformation emerged, tensions arose between church and state. Reformers like Martin Luther and William Tyndale challenged church authority, advocating for individual interpretation of Scripture. The church, fearing loss of control, responded with force, sparking conflicts and wars. States, too, began asserting independence, leading to power struggles.

Do you think that these powerful institutions, monarchies and nations decided to give up power and control?

Let's go back to what the world and its church will do to keep you in the dark.

Tyndale was led to the town square, where a stake had been prepared and was chained to it. The crowd gathered around, witnessing the final moments of a man who dared challenge the established order.

Before his execution, Tyndale uttered his famous last words: "Lord, open the King of England's eyes." These words echoed his unwavering dedication to spreading biblical truth.

He was then burned at the stake, a brutal conclusion to a life devoted to translating Scripture. The flames consumed his earthly form, but his legacy endured. Tyndale's ashes were scattered in the river Zenne, symbolizing the dispersal of his ideas.

Tyndale's execution served as a warning to others who dared challenge authority or share the truth.

His final words, "Lord, open the King of England's eyes," became a rallying cry for reformers.

Pause for a moment and reflect on your life and the world around you.

How are things going?

For many, the outlook is bleak. Wars, famine, and plagues ravage nations, while natural disasters leave communities broken and desperate. People are angry, bitter, and feeling alone. As you glance at the headlines, your heart sinks. The world seems to be Imploding, and hope appears lost.

The fabric of society is fraying. Economies teeter on the brink of collapse, and global tensions simmer. Fear grips the hearts of citizens as terrorism and violence escalate. The once-stable foundations of family, community and morality crumble beneath the weight of lies.

Wars displace millions, claiming countless lives. Famine grips nations, leaving families desperate. Locally, crime and poverty plague communities, fueling anger and division. The social fabric frays and society teeters on the brink of collapse.

Divorce rates soar, shattering families and leaving emotional rubble in their wake. Abuse and violence leave lasting scars, physical and emotional. Addiction holds lives hostage, ensnaring individuals in cycles of despair.

Friends and loved ones struggle with self-esteem, depression, and purpose, their inner worlds crumbling beneath the weight of expectation and uncertainty. Mental health crises escalate, overwhelming support systems and leaving individuals feeling isolated and adrift. The façade of confidence cracks, revealing fragile selves, uncertain and alone.

On a personal level, the struggle manifests as sleepless nights and weary days. Thoughts swirl, a relentless vortex of self-doubt and fear. Simple tasks become Herculean challenges and smiles hide the ache within. You see yourself stressed, overwhelmed, and alone, wondering how to cope with the crushing weight.

The mirror reflects a tired face, eyes sunken from lack of sleep, and a heart heavy with anxiety. Everyday conversations feel like minefields and social media amplifies the sense of inadequacy. The longing for connection and understanding grows, yet the fear of vulnerability and rejection holds you back.

In the middle of all this mess, we must ask, what is happening in our world? What is causing all of these problems? Which is to blame?

THE SIN DECEPTION

Of course, fingers point in every direction.

The media screams about corrupt leaders, flawed systems and social injustices. Politicians blame their opponents, while activists rail against institutions. It is always somebody's fault, and there is plenty of blame to go around.

It is the problem of greedy corporations that prioritize profits over people. Is it the Power-hungry politicians that sacrifice integrity for influence? It must be because social media amplifies hate speech and misinformation.

Yet, beneath all the noise, hidden out of sight, pushed down deep inside, and absolutely kept out of the spotlight is our problem.

But is this really the whole story? Are external forces solely responsible for our woes?

The truth is sin has always been the silent partner in humanity's downfall. From history's darkest moments to today's headlines, sin's fingerprints remain. It corrupts leaders, distorts systems and poisons relationships. The solution lies not in scapegoating external enemies but in confronting the internal adversary. Recognizing sin's insidious presence is the first step toward redemption and transformation.

Since humanity's dawn, sin has ravaged hearts, shattered relationships and destroyed lives. This endless struggle against darkness, selfishness and imperfection defines the human experience, transcending centuries and cultures.

Have you ever wondered why people do bad things or struggle with their flaws? For thousands of years, humans have grappled with sin. What is sin? Where does it come from? How does it infect relationships and societies? What's the root of this destructive force shackling humanity?

What if our understanding is flawed? What if the information guiding our decisions is incorrect? Misunderstanding sin has catastrophic consequences. Our grasp of human nature, morality and redemption hangs in the balance.

The stakes are high. Misguided perceptions spark a vicious cycle of guilt, shame and self-effort, trapping us in an endless struggle. Relationships suffer as complex individuals are reduced to simplistic labels, overlooking beauty and potential.

Misunderstanding sin prevents genuine transformation. Superficial behavioral changes merely treat symptoms, neglecting the root causes.

The cost of misunderstanding sin is too great to ignore.

Reconsidering our ideas about sin prompts us to reevaluate many of our fundamental beliefs. We're forced to confront questions about the nature of humanity: Are we inherently flawed, or are we created with inherent value? Does our worth stem from our actions, the things we do and don't do? This inquiry also raises questions about the source of morality. How do we know what is right and wrong? Is it based on rigid rules and regulations or something else?

Reexamining sin reveals God's character and our true identity. We see ourselves and others in a new light, valued and loved. This discovery brings liberation from guilt and shame, fostering empathy and compassion in our relationships. As we understand our place in

God's plan, we find purpose and passion in life. Uncovering the truth about sin sets us free, reflecting God's love and redemption in our lives and communities.

WALTER LEATHERS

Chapter 2

What is sin?

To grasp the essence of sin, we must explore its definitions and interpretations across cultures and traditions. Sin represents a universal human struggle, appearing in various forms. In Judaism, sin is viewed as a deviation from God's laws and commandments, emphasizing repentance and atonement. Islam understands sin as disobedience to Allah's will, separating individuals from divine guidance and mercy.

Across cultures, sin's implications are consistent. Hinduism sees sin as "papa" or "dharma," actions contrary to divine law governed by karma's law of cause and effect. Buddhism views sin as "kilesa" or mental defilements, obstacles to achieving enlightenment. Secular science perspectives, such as psychology and sociology, frame sin as harmful behaviors or choices damaging to oneself and others.

Despite cultural differences, universal truths emerge. Everyone has messed up, hurt others or been hurt. Sin separates us from loved ones and principles. Accountability matters, emphasizing responsibility. Murder, theft and deceit are universally recognized as wrong. The world recognizes sin's destructive power.

The biblical perspective provides the definitive, timeless and complete definition of sin. God's Word transcends human interpretations and cultural nuances, offering clear and authoritative insight. In "The Sin Deception," we'll delve into the biblical definition, exposing lies and half-truths. By returning to God's Word, we'll discover the liberating truth.

Our exploration begins in the Garden of Eden, where humanity's fateful mistake changed everything. What led Adam and Eve to disobey God? Was it a flaw within them or a clever deception? Understanding sin's roots reveals its harmful nature and profound impact on human history. Before sin's corrupting influence, life was different. Innocence, intimacy with God and potential were lost.

To effectively confront sin, we must distinguish between evil, the devil and sin. Are they the same or distinct forces? How do they interact? By clarifying these concepts, we'll overcome sin's grasp.

Chapter 3
The "7 Deadly Sins"

As we embark on this journey to understand sin, let's begin with a familiar starting point. Before diving into its complexities, let's revisit the timeless list of The 7 Deadly Sins. This ancient catalog of destructive tendencies - Pride, Envy, Wrath, Sloth, Greed, Gluttony, and Lust - has haunted humanity for centuries.

Documented early in history, these sins persist today, manifesting in harmful patterns that seem inescapable. Exploring these well-known transgressions will serve as a fitting warm-up for our deeper dive into sin's universal and pervasive nature.

By examining these seven sins, we'll begin to uncover the threads that weave sin into the fabric of our lives. This foundational understanding will prepare us for a more nuanced exploration of sin's complexities and its far-reaching consequences.

Pride

"Pride is the only disease that makes everyone sick except the person who has it."

Pride is a feeling of superiority or self-importance that can consume our thoughts and actions. It's an excessive confidence in our own abilities, accomplishments, or possessions. When pride takes over, it can lead to arrogance, entitlement, and a disregard for others.

Think about the person having a mindset where they believe they're better than everyone else. That's Pride, one of the 7 Deadly Sins. It's like building a luxury skyscraper around your ego, pushing humility out of the way.

In society, we often hear the term "narcissist" thrown around to describe someone who seems overly self-absorbed or arrogant. But what does it really mean to be a narcissist? Narcissistic personality disorder is a complex condition characterized by an excessive need for admiration, a sense of entitlement, and a lack of empathy for others. This is a person who constantly seeks praise, dominates conversations and expects special treatment without showing any genuine interest in others' feelings or needs. That's what narcissism looks like.

But here's the thing: narcissism and pride aren't exactly the same thing. Pride is the first and worst, at least in my opinion.

Narcissism, on the other hand, is driven by a deep-seated need for control and admiration. You know them; they are always wearing a mask that hides a fragile self-image. You know they appear confident, but beneath the surface, they're desperate for validation.

A Lie That Binds

For centuries, we've been taught that Adam and Eve's consumption of the forbidden fruit was the first sin.

But is this really the whole story?

Disobedience caused the destruction of everything.

Yes, it did, but not just disobedience… The heart is the real issue. The heart bent away from God.

The Pride Paradox – Unpacking the Church's Emphasis on Disobedience

The Bible attributes the first sin to pride, yet the church often focuses on disobedience. This disparity raises questions. Beloved, let's delve into the reasons behind this shift in focus.

Teaching disobedience as the first sin allows the church to focus on behavior, regulating actions while avoiding inner motivations. We can see how this approach enables the church to establish clear guidelines and maintain control. However, this comes at a cost.

By overemphasizing disobedience, the church overlooks the root causes of sin – pride and self-centeredness. We neglect personal growth, ignoring inner change for outward compliance. This fosters judgment, dividing people into "obedient" and "disobedient."

I want you to pause for a minute and think about that….

Dividing people by obedience or disobedience.

If you are taught to believe being disobedient is the problem, then you can be forced to do something about it.

If sin is primarily a matter of the heart, specifically pride, rather than mere disobedience, it profoundly impacts our understanding of faith. Recognizing sin as a heart issue emphasizes internal transformation over external compliance, shifting focus from adhering to rules to cultivating humility and love. This perspective contrasts with works-based religions, which prioritize external actions over inner transformation.

The consequences of misunderstanding sin are horrific. Legalism and self-righteousness emerge when obedience is overly emphasized. You make a list, and you check it twice now. You'll find out who's been naughty and who's been nice. Performance-based acceptance measures worth by achievements. Do you know what this looks like? It's a 30-day sober chip or a trophy for losing 20 lbs. It's a certificate recognizing 1 year of anger management.

Look at the impact in the real world that seeing sin as something to be worked away has.

n contrast, a heart-centered faith prioritizes humility, love-driven obedience and grace-based acceptance. This understanding redefines success, measuring faith by heart transformation, not external achievements.

Beloved, we can't work our way out of sin. You can't pray enough, fast enough or give enough to stop sin. You will never be good enough, no matter how hard you try and be.

That does not mean there isn't a solution for sin; there is. Hang in there.

The Bible reveals a startling truth: pride was the first sin committed long before humanity's fall. Lucifer's self-exaltation sparked a rebellion against God, forever altering the course of history **(Isaiah 14:12-15, Ezekiel 28:12-19).**

This original sin of pride set the stage for humanity's downfall.

When Satan tempted Eve, he exploited her desire for self-elevation, whispering, "You will be like God" *(Genesis 3:5).* But this wasn't the first sin – it was merely the first human sin.

The deception that the forbidden fruit was the first sin has obscured the true nature of pride's destructive power. By misunderstanding the origin of sin, we've underestimated the depth of pride's influence in our lives.

It's time to expose this lie that binds and confront the truth:

- Pride preceded human sin.
- Pride fueled Lucifer's rebellion.
- Pride manipulated Adam and Eve's choices.

Envy

"I'm not envious; I'm just intensely interested in your success."

– Unknown

Envy, the garden of resentment, where bitter roots produce poisonous fruit. Like a toxic garden, Envy chokes out gratitude and contentment, spreading toxic relationships and drama. Imagine a person scrolling through social media, fixated on a friend's seemingly perfect life, feeling resentment and entitlement.

Let me give you an example with The Unseen Struggle of Lily.

Lily, 16, seemed to have it all together. Her Instagram feed was filled with perfect selfies, trendy outfits, and happy moments with friends.

But behind the screen, Lily was drowning in envy.

She'd compare her life to her classmates' seemingly flawless existences, feeling inadequate and invisible.

"Why can't I be as popular as Emily?"

"Why doesn't anyone like my posts as much as Sarah's?"

"Why is everyone else's life so much better than mine?"

The constant comparison and feelings of inadequacy consumed Lily. She began to withdraw from friends and family, feeling like she couldn't measure up.

One fateful night, the pressure became too much. Lily made a devastating choice, leaving behind a trail of shattered dreams and unanswered questions.

The Reality

Lily's story is heartbreaking but not unique. According to the CDC, suicide rates among teenage girls have increased by 50% since 2017.

Envy, social media comparison, and the pressure to conform can be deadly.

Wrath

"Wrath begins where wisdom ends."

– Unknown

Wrath is a strong, intense anger or indignation, often leading to destructive consequences. It's an uncontrolled passion that can consume our thoughts and actions, causing harm to ourselves and others.

Imagine having a mindset where every slight feels like a personal attack, every delay a reason to rage. That's Wrath, one of the 7 Deadly Sins, forging a path of destruction through relationships, reputations, and lives.

Wrath can ignite in various forms, from fiery outbursts to simmering resentment, damaging connections and leaving scars. Chronic wrath can lead to strained relationships, poor physical health, and regrettable actions.

When we give in to wrath, we surrender to a toxic emotion that consumes our thoughts, words, and actions. This corruption can irreparably damage relationships, shatter trust, and leave lasting scars.

Moreover, human wrath is often fueled by selfishness, pride, and personal agendas rather than a genuine desire for justice or righteousness. This self-centeredness blinds us to the harm caused by our actions, making us incapable of administering fair judgment.

The Bible warns that human wrath "does not produce the righteousness that God desires" (James 1:20). Instead, it produces a cycle of violence, retaliation, and chaos. By indulging in wrath, we become agents of destruction rather than instruments of God's redeeming love.

Consider the devastating consequences of unchecked wrath. Take, for instance, the tragic example of school shooters. Fuelled by anger, resentment, and a desire for revenge, they unleash havoc on innocent lives. The aftermath leaves families shattered, communities traumatized, and society questioning how such evil could occur.

The Columbine massacre, the Sandy Hook tragedy, and other similar incidents demonstrate the horrific consequences of human wrath. These acts serve as stark reminders that uncontrolled anger and vengeance can have catastrophic effects.

Sloth

"Sloth: Because adulting is overrated."

*– **Unknown***

Sloth is a habit of indifference, apathy, and lethargy that can suffocate our potential and relationships. It's an excessive focus on comfort, convenience, and relaxation, often at the expense of responsibility, growth, and meaningful engagement.

Modern conveniences like food delivery apps, such as Grubhub, UberEats, and DoorDash, can lead to sloth. With just a few taps on our screens, we can have our favorite foods delivered to our doorsteps without exerting any physical effort. While this may seem harmless, it can reduce our motivation to engage in physical activity, cook healthy meals, or even leave our homes.

Another culprit is streaming services like Netflix, Hulu, and Amazon Prime. Binge-watching our favorite shows has never been easier, but excessive streaming can lead to a sedentary lifestyle, social isolation, and procrastination. Hours spent sitting and watching can turn into days, weeks, or even months of inactivity, causing us to neglect responsibilities, relationships, and personal growth.

Video games, for instance, can be a significant time-suck. According to a 2022 survey by the Entertainment Software

Association (ESA), 65% of American households have at least one gamer, and the average gamer spends around 14 hours per week playing games. This excessive gaming can lead to reduced physical activity, social isolation, and decreased productivity. A 2020 study by the Journal of Behavioral Addictions found that only 15% of gamers meet weekly exercise guidelines.

Excessive screen time is another culprit. On average, people worldwide spend around 6 hours and 40 minutes per day staring at screens, translating to approximately 46 hours and 40 minutes per week. In the United States, that number jumps to 7 hours and 3 minutes per day. This includes time spent on smartphones (2 hours and 21 minutes), tablets (37 minutes), and computers (42 minutes). Children and teens are particularly vulnerable, with 8-12-year-olds spending 5 hours and 33 minutes per day on entertainment screen time and 13-18-year-olds spending 8 hours and 39 minutes.

Does this mean that now I am saying, get up and stop scrolling. Is it time to work? No, it's not about what you do or don't do, but you should be aware that consequences are real, and everyone faces them eventually.

The consequences of excessive gaming and screen time are dire. Reduced physical activity increases the risk of obesity, diabetes, and cardiovascular disease.

Social isolation can lead to depression, anxiety, and decreased empathy. Decreased productivity affects work/school performance, relationships, and mental health.

When sloth takes over, it can lead to procrastination, demotivation, and a lack of purpose. Imagine having a mindset where you consistently prioritize temporary pleasure over lasting fulfillment. That's Sloth, one of the 7 Deadly Sins.

Greed

"I'm saving for a rainy day… or a private island."

Greed is an insatiable craving for wealth, possessions, or power that consumes our thoughts and actions. It's an excessive focus on material gain, often at the expense of relationships, ethics, and spiritual well-being. When greed takes over, it can lead to exploitation, manipulation, and a disregard for others' needs.

In popular culture, we're often told that "Greed is Good."

The infamous "Greed is Good" speech from the 1987 film Wall Street, delivered by Gordon Gekko (played by Michael Douglas), goes like this:

"Greed, for lack of a better word, is good. Greed is right. Greed works. Greed clarifies, cuts through, and captures the essence of the evolutionary spirit. Greed, in all of its forms—greed for life, money, love, and knowledge—has marked the upward surge of mankind.

"And greed—you mark my words—will not only save Teldar Paper but that other malfunctioning corporation called the USA.

"Greed is healthy. You can be greedy and still feel good about yourself."

This speech embodies the film's themes of excess, ambition and the morally ambiguous world of 1980s finance.

What are we being programmed to think about greed? Is it good? How can something that is a sin be good?

It's all about the money.

Money, money, money, MONEY!

We've been conditioned to believe that greed drives success, progress, and happiness.

Take OnlyFans, for instance. Creators sell explicit content, often blurring lines between intimacy and exploitation. The platform's top earners boast millions in annual income, perpetuating a culture of transactional relationships. Bella Thorne, a prominent OnlyFans creator, reportedly earned $11 million in just one week.

This phenomenon raises questions:

- What's the true cost of this "success"?
- Are we reducing human connection to a mere commodity?
- What values are we sacrificing for financial gain?

Gluttony

"Second breakfasts, and elevenses, and luncheon, and afternoon tea, and dinner, and supper!"

1. J.R.R. Tolkien, The Hobbit

Then, we have Gluttony, the bottomless pit of excess, where cravings consume us, and self-control is devoured. Like a voracious fire, Gluttony ravages our lives, leaving a trail of destruction and decay. Imagine a foodie obsessed with the next culinary thrill, indulging in lavish feasts and extravagant tastes yet never finding satisfaction. Gluttony leads to enslavement, as we become prisoners of our desires, sacrificing health, relationships, and dignity on the altar of fleeting pleasures.

Beloved, let me tell you about Natasha Owens.

Natasha Owens, a 45-year-old mother of two, struggled with gluttony and obesity her entire life. She turned to food for comfort, escapism, and coping with stress.

Despite her successful career as a marketing executive, Natasha felt ashamed of her body. She was constantly bombarded with societal beauty standards and unrealistic expectations.

In 2018, Natasha's weight reached 300 pounds. She developed diabetes, hypertension, and chronic pain. Her doctor warned her that her weight would significantly shorten her lifespan.

Natasha tried various diets, gym memberships, and weight loss programs but failed to sustain any progress. She felt like a failure.

Body dysmorphia consumed Natasha. She avoided mirrors, hid from cameras, and withdrew from social events.

In 2020, Natasha's mental health began to deteriorate. She experienced anxiety, depression, and suicidal thoughts.

On February 12, 2022, Natasha took her own life.

The reality that we must face is that Natasha's story highlights the devastating and far too common consequences of untreated gluttony, obesity, and body dysmorphia.

According to the CDC:

- 1 in 5 American adults struggle with obesity
- 30 million people in the US live with eating disorders
- Body dysmorphia affects 1 in 50 adults

Lust

"Lust is the only disease that can be spread by thinking about it."

Lust is a powerful and often overwhelming desire for physical pleasure or gratification. It can consume our thoughts and actions, leading us to prioritize instant satisfaction over emotional intimacy, relationships, and even our own well-being.

We're told that freedom equals being free to pursue our lust in any way we choose. Society bombards us with sensual imagery, normalizing objectification and sexualization. Advertisements use sex appeal to sell products, and pop culture glorifies casual sex and hedonism.

Have you ever seen an Axe body spray commercial? Do you remember the Carl's Jr. – Paris Hilton's "Spicy BBQ Burger" Commercial (2005)

It had Paris Hilton seductively washing a car and eating a burger.

I mean, come on, what is happening in the world?

Even baby products are marketed with sex appeal in mind. Huggies – "Daddy's Little Helper" Commercial (2012)

It Features attractive dads and babies in various playful and intimate moments.

Still not convinced sex sells? Check out these messages and think about the programming you are receiving.

- Burger King's "Subservient Chicken" Commercial (2004)

- Hardee's "Most American Thickburger" Commercial (2014)

These commercials sparked controversy and discussion about using sex to sell products. Ya think?

We have to be free to experience sex in all its variety, right? But what's the true cost of this "freedom"?

The sex-positive movement, meant to promote healthy attitudes, often prioritizes lust over intimacy and relationships. Hook-up culture and pressure to engage in casual sex can lead to emotional damage, relationship harm, and exploitation. Feminism's narrative of sexual freedom can overlook objectification and neglect the emotional aspects of sex.

Exposing the Lies that Bind: Free sex isn't free!

The modern idea of freedom has taken a troubling turn. We're led to believe that unlimited access to pornography, sexual exploration and lack of boundaries are the ultimate freedoms. But beneath this façade lies a disturbing reality.

Research reveals alarming consequences. Excessive pornography consumption can lead to decreased empathy, making us less sensitive to others' pain. It fuels aggression, contributes to violence, and distorts our views of relationships, eroding genuine intimacy.

Society often portrays high body counts and the "player" personality as cool and empowering. But this is a lie. Casual sex comes with severe consequences that affect our emotions, mental health and relationships.

Casual sex can lead to emotional trauma, causing hurt and exploitation. It increases anxiety, depression and low self-esteem. Physically, it puts us at risk of STDs, unintended pregnancies and weakened immune systems. Spiritually, it separates us from our values, faith and purpose.

This persona may seem glamorous, but it objectifies others for personal gain, fosters emotional numbness and avoids intimacy.

This redefined freedom masquerades as empowerment but actually exploits vulnerabilities, perpetuates harmful norms and distracts us from meaningful connections.

In today's popular culture, we're constantly bombarded with messages that normalize and even glorify lust. Music videos, movies, and social media platforms often objectify bodies, reduce relationships to mere physical encounters, and make instant gratification seem like the ultimate goal. We're led to believe that lust equals love, intimacy, or empowerment.

However, this couldn't be further from the truth. The rise of hookup culture and platforms like Tinder have created an environment where a physical connection is prioritized over an emotional one.

Pause for a moment and think about all the sex that happens between people who know nothing about one another,

Well, hopefully, they got a name at least…

Casual sex always leads to emotional emptiness, eventually.

The Alarming Truth About Hookup Culture

Beloved, I'm deeply concerned about the world we're living in. Hookup culture has become the norm, and it's having devastating effects on our mental and physical health, relationships and society as a whole.

Engaging in hookups and having multiple partners can lead to depression, anxiety and negative emotional outcomes. In fact, 82.6% of college students reported feeling embarrassed, losing respect and struggling to maintain steady relationships after hookups. Furthermore, 78% of women and 72% of men experienced regret afterward.

The rise of hookup culture has also led to an increase in STD transmission. Many young people mistakenly believe STDs are a thing of the past. Additionally, 77.8% of unwanted sex occurs in the context of hookups.

Hookup culture is also changing the way we approach relationships and marriage. Many young adults prioritize casual encounters over long-term commitments, leading to delayed marriages. The normalization of hookup culture reinforces the notion that committed love is unstable, potentially contributing to single-parent homes.

It's heartbreaking to see that over the past 60 years, traditional courting has been replaced by casual sexual encounters. Shockingly, 70% of sexually active 12-21-year-olds report having uncommitted sex within the last year.

Hello… is this thing on..?

Twelve-year-olds having casual sex? What in the world is happening

The 7 Deadly Sins represent some of the most destructive and universal human temptations, but they're only a starting point for understanding sin's complexity.

Before we go, we should see how the church uses "pride" to make money and hold on to power.

Pride, yes, one of the 7 Deadly Sins we just studied, has significant economic implications, particularly within religious institutions and powerful governments.

The church historically sold indulgences to forgive sins, including pride, generating an estimated annual revenue of $100 million to $500 million in the pre-Reformation era.

Churches collect donations, partly driven by pride in supporting the institution, with estimated annual revenues ranging from $100 billion to $500 billion globally. Religious tourism, driven by pride in faith, generates $50 billion to $100 billion annually.

The sale of pride-themed merchandise, such as apparel and accessories, contributes an estimated $100 million to $500 million annually. Additionally, wealthy individuals donate to gain prestige and recognition, with estimated annual revenues between $1 billion and $5 billion.

The church utilizes pride to reinforce its hierarchical structure, with clergy authority bolstered by pride. Rituals and ceremonies foster pride, while symbolism, iconography, art and architecture evoke pride in faith. Community building and fundraising efforts also leverage pride.

Critics argue that the church exploits pride for financial gain, perpetuating social hierarchies and materialism that undermine spiritual values. Again, Ya think?

Some 37% of Americans donate to religious organizations, according to Gallup. The global religious market is projected to reach $4.2 trillion by 2025, reports ResearchAndMarkets.

The intersection of pride and economics raises complex questions about the role of institutions in shaping human values and behaviors.

Does the world profit off of pride, too? Of course, every sin can be exploited for profit, power and control.

LGBT Pride has evolved into a significant economic force, influencing various industries and communities. The annual Pride month celebrations and parades generate substantial revenue through tourism and travel, attracting millions of visitors worldwide and injecting billions into local economies. Key destinations like New York City, San Francisco and Miami see significant boosts in tourism revenue.

Major corporations invest heavily in Pride sponsorships, advertising and branding, reaching a lucrative and loyal LGBT market. Estimated annual spending exceeds $1 billion. Pride-themed merchandise, from apparel to accessories, generates hundreds of millions in revenue. Companies capitalize on the trend, offering branded products.

Entrepreneurs have created LGBT-focused businesses catering to the community's needs and preferences. This niche market contributes significantly to local economies. Companies embracing LGBT inclusivity attract top talent, improve employee satisfaction and enhance their brand reputation. Diversity and inclusion initiatives have become essential for business success.

The LGBT community's purchasing power exceeds $1.4 trillion annually, according to the National Gay and Lesbian Chamber of Commerce. Pride events generate $1.1 billion in economic impact, as reported by NYC Pride. LGBT tourism contributes $65 billion to the US economy, per the US Travel Association.

Critics argue that corporate involvement overshadows the movement's social justice roots, while companies face accusations of exploiting LGBT issues for marketing gain. Debate surrounds the representation and support of marginalized LGBT subgroups.

The economic influence of LGBT Pride is substantial, with 71% of LGBT individuals preferring brands supporting LGBT causes, according to Harris Poll. Sixty-one percent of Americans support LGBT rights, reports Pew Research. The global LGBT market is projected to reach $5.5 trillion by 2025, states ResearchAndMarkets.

Wow. That is a lot of money and power.

Beloved, the kingdom of sin, makes a lot of money off of sin.

For brevity's sake, I am going to forgo illustrating the profit and power behind the other deadly sins but rest assured, together, these deadly 7 sins control the world.

We know what sin looks like now, but what is sin?

The definition of Sin is a complex one that people can't seem to agree on. Different cultures, religions, and personal experiences lead to varying views. Even language and human nature add to the confusion.

Think of it like trying to define "right" and "wrong." Some believe it's absolute, while others think it depends on the situation. This debate makes it hard to pin down what sin really means.

Without a clear understanding, sin can be difficult to recognize and address. It's like trying to find a moving target. When right and wrong are unclear, people may justify harmful actions or deceive themselves.

Think about "pride" .. is pride a good thing or a bad thing?

To comprehend the elusive concept of sin, we should first acknowledge the limitations of human understanding. Our perceptions of sin are shaped by various influences: personal experiences, cultural norms, philosophical theories, and scientific discoveries. However, these perspectives often provide incomplete or conflicting views.

As Blaise Pascal astutely observed, "The darkness of sin is a darkness of the mind, and it is a darkness that cannot be dispelled by mere reason or knowledge." Our individual struggles with sin can lead to subjective interpretations, self-justification, and despair.

Tim Keller wisely noted, "If you don't understand the nature of sin, you won't understand the nature of salvation."

Chapter 4
The Hidden Truth of Sin: Unveiling the church's Intentional Deception.

When we allow the church to define sin, historically, we get exploitation for power and wealth!

For centuries, Christianity's most revered institutions have shaped our understanding of right and wrong. We have trusted them to tell us what is sin and what isn't.

But what if our churches intentionally distorted the concept of sin to serve their own interests?

The church's definition of sin has been shrouded in mystery, with interpretations varying across denominations and cultures. But what if this ambiguity conceals a deliberate attempt to manipulate us?

How can something be a sin today but not tomorrow? How can something that is a sin be given an indulgence? If I can sin with no consequence, does sin even matter? Can't I just go to confession, say a few Hail Marys and be good? Doesn't my tithe cover that stuff?

What if the church's portrayal of sin prioritizes control over spiritual growth?

As we continue to explore this puzzle, we'll expose the church's intentional deception and uncover the authentic meaning of sin.

Beloved, some of you will be hurt to learn this, but be open-minded and understand Jesus is our Savior, not the church. Stick with me as we unravel the tangled threads of sin, revealing the church's hidden agenda and reclaiming the truth that has been obscured for centuries.

Before you think I'm criticizing the Church or encouraging abandoning your spiritual home, hold on a little longer…

let's expose a crucial truth by exposing Another Lie that Binds

The world portrays **Jesus as the leader** of various religions, but is that true? Is Jesus the head of all of these various churches?

Recently, Pope Francis, the head of the Catholic church, said, "All religions are paths to reach God."

How can this be?

Religions worldwide, with very differing practices, all claim Jesus as their leader. Churches with all kinds of different names and "statements " of faith all claim their religion is the right religion. How can that be? More importantly, which religion is Jesus the leader of?

Beloved, it doesn't matter.

Whatever your religion is, Jesus is opposed to it!

Read that again:

Whatever your religion is, Jesus is opposed to it!

The world and the church, with a lowercase "c" perpetuate a

misleading narrative: Jesus as a religious leader.

However, biblical truth reveals Him as the cornerstone of our personal relationship with God, not the grand poobah of some religions.

Think about the Jesus of the Bible for a minute.

Jesus' teachings challenged the religious norms of His time. He criticized the Pharisees and Sadducees for prioritizing rituals and traditions over genuine faith and compassion. Jesus emphasized a personal connection with God, stressing love, forgiveness and humility.

Religion focuses on rituals, rules and institutions, whereas a relationship with God emphasizes personal connection, trust and surrender. Jesus' teachings encouraged individuals to move beyond mere religiosity and engage in a meaningful, dynamic relationship with God.

The Church can play a vital role in fostering this relationship but not until it's understood that Jesus didn't establish Himself as a leader within organized religion. Instead, He founded The Church – a community of believers, with Himself as the Head *(Ephesians 5:23, Colossians 1:18)*. This distinction is crucial.

In contrast to rigid religiosity, Jesus emphasizes a vibrant, direct connection with God. He critiques empty traditions and rituals, prioritizing love, forgiveness and humility *(Matthew 23:13-36, Mark 7:1-23).* The Church, comprised of believers, serves as a catalyst for spiritual growth, fostering intimacy and transformation.

Beloved, the difference is everything.

The church of the world doesn't want you to have a direct relationship with God; if you do, they lose control.

It has been said that Jesus was the most anti-religious person to ever walk the earth.

Let's recap the differences. A church Under Sin's Dominion and the Church Headed by Christ!

The word "Church" can be misleading, encompassing both the global community of believers in Jesus Christ and the church (lowercase) institutions governed by sin's influence.

To recognize the difference, start with what the Bible defines as the Church.

The Greek word "Ἐκκλησία" (Ekklesia) defines the Church as "those called out" or "the called-out ones," emphasizing its distinct purpose. The Church is called out from the world, in it but not part of it.

Beloved, if your church looks just like the world… it's a church with a lowercase c.

When the world enters the church, destruction, deception and devastation follow. When the Church enters the world, love, charity and compassion come with it.

The authentic Church, headed by Christ the Savior, comprises believers united in faith, following biblical teachings, seeking inner transformation and embodying Christ's love and redemption. This Church prioritizes spiritual growth, inner transformation and Christ-centered leadership.

The Church is all about loving God and loving their neighbor.

The Bible promises that you will know them… the real Church, by their love.

In contrast, institutions masquerading as the Church often fall prey to sin's dominion. These are not Church's battling sin, not waging war against sin, not claiming rightful dominion over sin. These are the compromised churches, the surrendered churches; these are the all-inclusive Sunday show churches. These entities prioritize power and wealth, distort biblical teachings, focus on external behavior and perpetuate fear and control. Their leadership is human-centered, the purpose is institutional power and the theology is marked by fear and control.

I did a quick Google search and look what came up.

Here is the list of the holdings of several different churches. Different churches!

1. The Church of Jesus Christ of Latter-day Saints - $16 billion
2. Catholic Church - $15 billion
3. Church of England - $10 billion
4. Baptist Church - $6 billion
5. Methodist Church - $5 billion

What do these things have in common? Billions of dollars. They are all worth Billions.

Beloved, I am not saying religious leaders should be poor, but The extraordinary wealth that these people have …..

When compared with the extraordinary need that exists….

I don't think so… I mean…… what would Jesus do?

- The world's top 10 pastors collectively hold over $1 billion in wealth.
- 1 in 7 people globally live in poverty, exceeding 1 billion individuals.
- 821 million people suffer from hunger.

Until we recognize this distinction, we can not reclaim the authentic Church, the one that aligns with Christ's teachings and purpose. We must discern the difference between the true Church and those hijacked by sin, ensuring our faith remains rooted in biblical truth.

The consequences of confusing these two entities are severe. Believers risk being misled, spiritual growth is stifled, and the Church's reputation suffers.

While local Churches and denominations can offer valuable guidance, they aren't the ultimate authority on sin. Only the Bible provides a comprehensive understanding of sin, rooted in God's character and design for humanity. As the apostle Paul said, "The Scriptures are the breath of God, and they are useful for teaching, rebuking, correcting, and training in righteousness" *(2 Timothy 3:16).*

For centuries, the Bible has been a cornerstone of Western civilization, offering historical insights, cultural context, and spiritual guidance. Its historical narrative is corroborated by archaeological findings and extrabiblical evidence.

THE SIN DECEPTION

The Bible alone offers a clear definition of sin, untainted by human error. In contrast, the church has often perpetuated sin's darkness, contradicting biblical teachings.

Historical examples might include condemning harmless behaviors and accepting sinful practices. What happens when the definition of sin is always changing?

We don't know what is right or wrong, what is a sin and what isn't.

The church's condemnation of left-handedness is a striking example. During the Middle Ages, left-handedness was viewed as a sign of demonic possession or evil intentions. Many left-handed children were forced to switch to right-handedness, leading to unnecessary suffering.

Some Christian denominations thought dancing was wrong. They believed it was sinful because they misunderstood some parts of the Bible.

Being able to dance is a gift of God; ask anyone who can't dance anymore.

Still this misunderstanding made lots of people think dancing was evil.

The iconic movie Footloose (1984), starring Kevin Bacon, comes to mind. Set in a small town where dancing is banned, Reverend Shaw Moore cites selective scripture to justify his stance, claiming dance corrupts youth. Ren McCormack, played by Kevin Bacon, boldly challenges this ban.

In a pivotal scene, Ren engages Reverend Moore, referencing 2 Samuel 6:14 (ESV): "David danced before the Lord with all his might... Michal, Saul's daughter, saw King David leaping and dancing before the Lord, and she despised him in her heart." Ren emphasizes, "See, Reverend, David danced with joy; the Bible doesn't condemn it. Michal despised him due to fear of others' opinions."

This powerful exchange showcases Ren's determination to challenge the status quo, demonstrating dance can be a form of worship and praise. Ironically, Reverend Moore mirrors Michal, whom the Bible condemns for her judgmental attitude.

Can the kingdom of sin pervert dancing, a form of praise to sin? Of course, that is the point.

What God gave for good, sin perverts for harm.

This isn't just a movie plot; in real life, some Christian leaders have made mistakes like this, too. They've banned music, making people feel scared, ashamed, or restricted.

You can hear the old person yelling now, "Stop playing that noise. ".

Certain Christian groups have banned modern music, restricting worship to traditional hymns, Psalms or a cappella singing. These groups aim to maintain traditional practices, separate from worldly influences and prioritize biblical purity.

Those sound like really good reasons, and perhaps they are, but their stance raises important questions:

THE SIN DECEPTION

Are musical rules diverting attention from celebrating the Lord?

Do guidelines reflect a complete understanding of sin and redemption?

Are rules rooted in biblical principles or misguided interpretations?

Are external regulations avoiding confrontation with the heart?

Again, can the kingdom of sin use music to entrap people? Of course, that is the point.

But ask yourself why it always comes down to what you do or don't do.

The difference between dancing before the Lord in praise and grinding on the dance floor for attention is stark and controlled entirely by the heart. As always, sin is a heart issue.

Let's clarify how sin can pervert anything God has created. Do you know what the weapon of choice the serpent first used to tempt man? Food.

Yes, beloved, the kingdom of sin uses food against us. Sin corrupts everything.

The Church's betrayal of biblical teachings on sin is a deliberate distortion driven by a desire for power and control. By redefining sin, the Church asserts authority over believers' lives, controlling their thoughts and actions. This intentional deception prioritizes institutional power over spiritual truth, shielding the Church's status quo.

Fear and misguidance also fuel this betrayal.

They are afraid you will open your eyes to the lies that bind.

The Church misinterprets scripture to protect believers from perceived threats, reinforcing fear rather than faith. Personal agendas and cultural norms are prioritized over biblical principles, further distorting the truth.

Think about the recent divisions in all of these worldly churches. Splitting up over gay marriage and female pastors, destroying themselves over abortion and politics. The consequences of this intentional betrayal are severe. The church is divided, spiritual growth is hindered, and believers are misled.

I know more churches hurt people than you could ever imagine. People are wounded by people in a house pretending to be of the Lord. I am not talking about minor slights or offenses; I am talking about people who turned to the church and found judgment and condemnation, not Love.

Lest you think these are just minor things, dancing and music and old wives tales about being left-handed, let me share a much darker lie perpetuated by the church.

The church's acceptance of slavery is a dark chapter in its history. Many Christian leaders and churches supported slavery, citing biblical passages to justify the ownership of human beings. This egregious error perpetuated racism and oppression.

The Bible's stance on slavery is often misrepresented. In reality, it advocates for equality and inherent human value. All individuals are created equal, bearing God's image and establishing dignity and worth regardless of race, status or background.

This fundamental principle is reinforced through teachings emphasizing spiritual equality, such as the unity of believers in Christ. Biblical laws regulated existing societal structures, aiming to humanize and limit slavery.

However, the church, with a lowercase "c," historically perpetuated slavery. Many churches accumulated wealth through the slave trade and ownership. Yes, beloved, the church benefited from slavery.

One notable example is the donation made by John Newton, a British slave trader turned abolitionist, to the Church of England.

In 1788, Newton donated a significant portion of his wealth, accumulated from his slave trading activities, to the Church of England to establish the Church Missionary Society.

Approximately £1,000 (equivalent to £120,000 today)

Newton's experiences as a slave trader led him to become an abolitionist. He later wrote the hymn "Amazing Grace" and advocated against slavery.

He is not the only one. If you saw a list of the sources of the money laundered through the church historically, you might cry.

Other notable examples include:

- The Catholic Church received donations from slave owners and traders in the Americas during the colonial era.
- The Anglican Church benefited from slave-based wealth in the

Caribbean.

Some churches even used biblical passages to justify slavery, ignoring the inherent value and dignity of enslaved individuals. This misguided interpretation enriched the church institutionally but compromised its moral authority.

The consequences of this deception linger, affecting marginalized communities.

Ask yourself how these people, who control the scripture and lecture others, could read the Word of God and still believe that you can chase God and at the same time drag along a slave in chains.

They weren't mistaken or misled…. They chose the kingdom of sin.

The Church, with a capital C, still has a critical role in confronting sin. However, the first requirement is the understanding of sin grounded in Scripture. By embracing the Bible's authority, we can uncover the entire truth about sin and all its complexities.

The Church has often struggled to maintain its distinctiveness, becoming entangled with the world's values and practices. Jesus taught, "My kingdom is not of this world" *(John 18:36),* yet the Church has frequently conformed to worldly standards.

This conformity has led to a watered-down gospel, prioritizing temporal success over eternal impact. The Church has become indistinguishable from the world, failing to provide a countercultural alternative.

To fulfill its calling, the Church must rediscover its identity as "those called out." This requires embracing its sacred mandate to confront sin while avoiding the world's corrupting influence. By clinging to Scripture and the Holy Spirit's guidance, the Church can regain its very important voice.

Ultimately, the Bible – not the Church – holds the key to understanding sin. As believers, we must anchor our faith in Scripture, ensuring the Church remains a beacon of hope in a sin-scarred world.

Chapter 5

Sin, Evil & Satan – Understanding the Distinctions

The Oxford definition of "sin" – "an act or thought that is considered wrong or immoral" – only scratches the surface. To truly comprehend sin, we must distinguish it from evil and Satan.

The Definition of Sin – Historical, Worldly and Modern Perspectives

The definition of sin has evolved significantly across historical, worldly and modern contexts, reflecting differing views on human nature, morality and divine authority.

Historically, the Christian church viewed sin as a serious offense against God, violating His commandments and divine sovereignty. This perspective emphasized humanity's inherent sinful nature, resulting from Adam and Eve's fall in Eden. Sin was seen as a rebellion against God, leading to spiritual death, separation from Him and a need for redemption through Jesus Christ. The early church fathers, such as Augustine and Aquinas, reinforced this understanding.

In contrast, the worldly view sees sin as relative, subjective and culturally defined. This perspective often dismisses the concept of sin or redefines it as personal flaws or mistakes. It emphasizes human autonomy, freedom and self-expression, downplaying accountability to divine authority.

Modern worldly churches often adopt a more nuanced view, blending biblical teachings with secular perspectives. They may redefine sin as social injustices, inequality or personal struggles, shifting focus from individual accountability to collective responsibility. This approach emphasizes God's love and acceptance over His judgment and sovereignty.

The forever and always unchanging Biblical Definition!

Sin, derived from the Hebrew "חֵטְא" (chet'), means "to miss the mark." It represents a deliberate deviation from God's intended path, rejecting His sovereignty and authority. Sin encompasses disobeying God's will, disregarding His commandments and separating ourselves from Him, resulting in spiritual death, relational brokenness, emotional turmoil and physical suffering.

Comparing these perspectives reveals significant differences. The historical church views sin as a rebellious act against God, while the worldly perspective sees sin as relative or nonexistent. Modern worldly churches redefine sin, emphasizing social justice. Understanding these contrasting views helps clarify the complexities surrounding sin and its implications for faith, morality and personal growth.

Evil

Evil is the consequence of sin – the darkness and suffering that result from our disobedience. It manifests as suffering, injustice, oppression, and destruction.

Satan

Satan, the fallen angel, tempts us to sin and deceives us with lies. However, he is not the embodiment of sin itself but a separate entity with limited power. The origin of sin lies within humanity's heart, not in Satan's influence.

Conflating sin, evil, and Satan can lead to misguided thinking, obscuring our understanding of God's character and the nature of sin. Recognizing these distinctions empowers us to confront our rebellion and seek redemption.

Beloved, Sin is the inclination of our rebellious heart bent away from God. While evil is the consequence of sin, think of evil as the fruit of wickedness that is sin.

- Satan: The tempter who seeks to lead us into sin.

Let's Employ a Powerful Analogy to Illuminate Sin's Complexities

I want you to think about sin as a person, place, and thing for a moment. It will help us to grasp its nature and consequences. Inspired by Jesus' parables, this creative framework expands our perception of sin, revealing its subtle influences.

Sin as a person highlights its destructive power and seductive allure. It operates like a clever foe, tempting and deceiving us. By recognizing its tactics, we empower ourselves to resist. This perspective exposes sin's cunning nature, helping us develop strategies to overcome its influence.

Envisioning sin as a place reveals its environmental impact. Just as certain environments foster growth or decay, sin's presence corrupts and destroys. This analogy aids in identifying areas where sin takes root, enabling us to create boundaries and protect ourselves.

Considering sin as a thing – an object or entity – exposes its inherent value and appeal. Sin often masquerades as something desirable, hiding its true nature. This insight enables us to evaluate desires and choices more critically, discerning between genuine goodness and deceptive allure.

By employing this analogy, we gain a more complete understanding of sin, empowering us to confront its destructive nature. Throughout our exploration, we'll return to this framework, unpacking its implications and deepening our understanding of sin's complexities. Again, bear with me and imagine sin as a:

Person

Thinking of sin as a person helps us understand its personal and relational aspects. Sin is often depicted as a tempter, accuser, and deceiver, seeking to separate us from God's love. It's a force that can seduce, manipulate, and enslave us, leading us away from God's design and purpose.

Place

Envisioning sin as a place helps us comprehend its environmental and cultural dimensions. Sin can create a toxic atmosphere that pollutes our surroundings, influencing our thoughts, words, and actions. It can also shape our cultural norms, values, and beliefs, perpetuating darkness and evil.

Idea

Conceptualizing sin as an idea highlights its intellectual and philosophical aspects. Sin is a twisted ideology that distorts our understanding of truth, beauty, and goodness. It's a corrupting influence that can deceive our minds and hearts, leading us to exchange God's truth for lies.

The Kingdom Of Sin

Finally, imagining sin as a kingdom helps us grasp its systemic and structural dimensions. Sin is a ruling power that seeks to dominate and enslave humanity, perpetuating a kingdom of darkness and evil. It's a force that can infiltrate and corrupt every level of society, from individual hearts to global systems.

The "Kingdom of Sin" will be a major theme as we move forward because understanding it is foundational to understanding sin.

By recognizing sin in its entirety, we can better understand its impact on our lives and the world around us.

What is sin, really? Is it a mistake, a weakness, or a rebellion against something greater than ourselves? Perspectives on sin vary widely, depending on one's beliefs. Understanding sin is crucial as it shapes our actions, decisions, and worldviews.

From a secular perspective, sin can be understood as a betrayal of our highest human potential, a failure to cultivate empathy, compassion, and wisdom. It's the accumulation of harmful choices, perpetuating suffering and injustice, and neglecting our responsibility to ourselves, others, and the world around us. Some view sin as a personal choice, while others see it as an inherent trait, a social construct, or a cultural norm.

Non-believers often define sin as "a flaw I was born with," "a personal weakness," or "a natural part of being human." This perspective sees sin as a noun – an inherent trait, a genetic predisposition, or a natural aspect of human nature. Consequently, solutions to sin focus on human effort and work: self-improvement, social reform, or cultural shifts.

The contrast between the world's view and the biblical view is striking. Secular perspectives attribute sin to human nature or circumstance, while the Bible traces sin to humanity's rebellion against God. The world sees sin as a fixed trait or inherent flaw, whereas the Bible views sin as a choice, an action, or a state of being.

Furthermore, the consequences of sin differ significantly between these two perspectives. The world often minimizes sin's consequences, while the Bible warns of spiritual death, separation from God, and eternal judgment.

A Christian might say, "I sinned by lying to my friend," acknowledging the action as a deliberate choice that requires confession and forgiveness.

On the other hand, a non-believer might say, "I was just joking, or that is just what I heard." viewing sin as an Inherent flaw rather than a deliberate action. Just a minor thing, nothing really.

Have you ever observed how people perceive their mistakes differently? Consider infidelity, for example.

The Bible teaches that a believer should acknowledge, "I cheated, and it was wrong. I chose to betray my spouse's trust, and now I must confess and seek forgiveness."

In contrast, a non-believer might rationalize, "It didn't mean anything; it was just a hookup."

Society goes even further and often encourages denial, reminiscent of Shaggy's infamous lyrics, "It wasn't me!" This stark contrast highlights the divergence in accountability and self-reflection.

This pattern repeats with addiction. A Christian might acknowledge, "I struggled with alcoholism, but I recognize it as a sin. I made choices that led me here, and now I need to seek help and forgiveness." Meanwhile, a non-believer might shift the blame, saying, "I'm an addict because of genetics and environment. It's not my fault; it's just who I am." Or, "My dad was an alcoholic, so I inherited it."

The same disparity shows up with anger issues. A Bible believer should take responsibility, saying, "I lost my temper and yelled at my kids. That was wrong, and I need to apologize. Jesus calls me to be better."

On the other hand, a person might attribute it to circumstances, saying, "I have anger issues because of childhood trauma. It's just part of my personality."

These contrasting views reveal fundamentally different understandings of sin and personal responsibility. One perspective acknowledges sin as a choice, requiring confession and forgiveness. The other shifts blame to nature, nurture, or circumstance, dodging accountability.

These examples demonstrate the distinct perspectives:

Biblical View: Sin is a deliberate choice, requiring confession, forgiveness, and personal responsibility.

The world view: Sin is an inherent flaw, often attributed to factors like genetics, environment, or circumstance.

Morals are the foundation of our decisions and interactions, distinguishing right from wrong. But what shapes these principles? The world and the Bible approach morality differently.

In the Bible, morality is rooted in God's character. The Bible teaches morals as objective truth. We can clearly determine right from wrong, based on God'sunchanging declaration.

The world, on the other hand, teaches us to rely on personal conscience, cultural norms, social contracts, and philosophical frameworks like humanism or utilitarianism. Their moral compass is influenced by reason, experience, and culture.

A key difference between these perspectives lies in their source: Believers derive morality from scripture, while the world draws from reason, experience, and culture. Again, the Bible teaches that moral truths are absolute, whereas the world often sees them as relative. Accountability also differs, with Christians believing in divine accountability and non-believers focusing on human consequences.

In stark contrast, biblical morals offer a timeless and absolute foundation for ethics. Rooted in the character of God, these principles emphasize love, justice, and compassion. The Bible teaches that human life has inherent dignity and worth, created in God's image. This profound truth underscores the importance of respecting and valuing every individual.

Moreover, biblical morals recognize the inherent flaw in human nature, acknowledging that our hearts can be deceitful and prone to sin.

By embracing biblical morals, we can anchor our values in an unchanging and divine standard.

As you can plainly see, a striking distinction emerges. Christians typically view sin as a verb – an action, a choice, a deliberate departure from God's will. In contrast, the world often perceives sin as a noun – a state, a condition, an inherent aspect of human nature. This fundamental difference has far-reaching implications.

Chapter 6

Sin As A Noun

A person, place or thing

The first mention of the actual word "sin" in the Bible is in Genesis 4:7, which states:

"If you do well, will you not be accepted? And if you do not do well, sin is crouching at the door. Its desire is for you, but you must rule over it."

Notice that sin is first used as a **noun** in the Bible.

When we discuss sin, we often struggle to define it. Is it a noun, a person, a place, a thing, or an idea?

The answer is yes, . Sin is a noun – a naming word representing a concrete or abstract entity.

Remember, sin is like a person but not a person. It has a presence, influencing thoughts and actions, yet lacks human form. The Bible describes sin as a "power" that enslaves (Romans 6:6) and a "tempter" that lures (1 Thessalonians 3:5). Sin's personal nature makes it relatable yet distinct from human identity.

Again, it's sin's personal nature that makes it relatable and intimate, striking at the very core of individual vulnerabilities. It's a universal human experience that resonates deeply as each person struggles with their unique temptations and weaknesses. Sin seeps into the cracks of our lives, exploiting our deepest fears, desires, and insecurities. This personal aspect of sin acknowledges the internal battles we face, where moral agency and choice intersect with our frailties.

Because sin targets each person precisely where they are most vulnerable, it can be particularly deceptive and insidious.

Sin is more than just a mistake or a slip-up. It's an environment that separates us from God, described as "darkness" (John 3:19) and "exile" (Psalm 107:4-7), affecting our relationships and choices.

Sin is more than just a thought or feeling. It's a corrupting influence that distorts truth and values (Romans 1:25), shaping cultures and worldviews.

Sin is more than just a personal struggle. It's a kingdom, a domain of rebellion against God, with its own "prince" – the ruler of this world (John 12:31) – and its own "citizens" (Ephesians 2:2-3). We once lived under its influence, driven by our passions and desires, and were naturally children of wrath, just like the rest of humanity.

Sin's presence is evident in everyday moments:

We gossip about a friend, rationalizing it as harmless chatter.

We prioritize social media likes over meaningful relationships.

We indulge in excessive consumption, ignoring the needs of others.

We harbor grudges, refusing to forgive.

We deceive ourselves, believing "white lies" are acceptable.

Sin is more than just these common transgressions. It's a fundamental orientation away from God, manifesting in various forms.

The Bible defines sin as any thought, action, or attitude that violates God's commands (1 John 3:4, ESV: "Everyone who makes a practice of sinning also practices lawlessness; sin is lawlessness."). It's anything that falls short of God's perfect standard (Romans 3:23, ESV: "for all have sinned and fall short of the glory of God").

But sin is complex. Sometimes, it's overt, like lying or stealing. Other times, it's subtle, like neglecting to help someone in need or harboring wrong thoughts. The Bible distinguishes between commission (actively doing something wrong) and omission (passively not doing something right). Attitudinal sins, like hatred or envy, can be just as destructive.

To grasp the complexity of sin, it's essential to examine three crucial aspects: intent, context, and consequences. Intent refers to the motivation or purpose behind an action or thought. Context considers the circumstances and environment that led to the behavior. Consequences encompass the impact on oneself and others. Analyzing these factors helps identify sin's presence and its effects.

However, two significant obstacles can hinder the recognition of sin: habituation and rationalization. Habituation occurs when repeatedly engaging in sinful patterns makes them seem normal or acceptable, dulling awareness of their harmful nature. Rationalization involves making excuses or justifying wrong behavior, deceiving oneself into believing it's not a sin. This self-deception can lead individuals to downplay or dismiss their wrongdoing.

Recognizing these dynamics is vital to understanding sin's influence. By acknowledging intent, context, and consequences and being aware of habituation and rationalization, we can develop a clearer understanding of sin's presence in our lives.

Thankfully, Scripture provides guidance. By studying biblical teachings on sin, listening to the Holy Spirit's conviction, and seeking feedback from fellow believers, we can identify areas where we have gone astray. Prayerfully asking God to reveal my sin helps me grow in self-awareness.

When we think of sin, we often reduce it to a simple choice – a mistake, a lapse in judgment, or a momentary weakness. But sin is far more sinister. It's a dark, rebellious force that defies God's authority, seeking to undermine His will and dominate every aspect of human existence.

Sin is not just a poor decision.

Beloved, sin is a malevolent power that opposes God's love, wisdom, and justice. It corrupts relationships, distorts thinking, and enslaves individuals to its destructive desires. Sin's influence is insidious, seeping into every crevice of our lives, often undetected.

Consider the hidden sins that can ravage our souls: self-righteousness, unforgiveness, bitterness, resentment, fear, anxiety, comparison, people-pleasing, and perfectionism. These subtle yet destructive forces can masquerade as virtues, making it difficult to recognize their true nature. But make no mistake, they are sin – and they are deadly.

Sin's ultimate goal is to separate us from God's love and redemption. It whispers lies, fuels doubts, and amplifies fears, slowly eroding our faith and confidence in God. Sin seeks to reduce us to slaves, bound by its oppressive chains, rather than children of God, empowered by His grace.

The Bible warns us that sin is a power that enslaves (Romans 6:6) and a tempter that lures (1 Thessalonians 3:5). It's a force that must be acknowledged and resisted, not merely recognized as a poor choice. When we trivialize sin, we underestimate its destructive potential.

Don't be deceived – sin is more than a choice. It's a formidable foe that seeks to dominate and destroy.

The Bible paints a stark picture of sin, portraying it as a relentless and formidable adversary. In Isaiah 57:20-21, we're told, "The wicked are like the tossing sea, which cannot rest… There is no peace, says my God, for the wicked." This vivid imagery conveys the turbulent and restless nature of sin, perpetually stirring up chaos and destruction.

Further emphasizing sin's hostile nature, Romans 8:7 states, "The mind of the flesh is hostile to God. It does not submit to God's law; indeed, it cannot." This passage highlights the fundamental opposition between sin and God, underscoring the impossibility of reconciling the two.

On a broader scale, 1 John 5:19 reveals that the entire world is under the influence of evil, declaring, "We know that we are children of God and that the whole world is under the control of the evil one." This sobering reality underscores the pervasive reach of sin, affecting every aspect of our lives and surroundings.

Together, these passages demonstrate that sin is a powerful and unrelenting force, opposed to God's will and destructive in its consequences.

As a power opposed to God, Sin blinds us to God's truth and love, preventing us from seeing and experiencing the fullness of His character.

Sin tempts us to prioritize ourselves over others, leading us down a path of selfishness and isolation. It fosters pride, greed, and ambition, which consume our thoughts and actions and corrupt our motivations.

Through its influence, Sin corrupts our relationships and communities, causing division, strife, and hurt. Ultimately, Sin leads us away from God's purpose and plan for our lives, distracting us from our true calling and destiny.

Once again, let's consider sin as a noun, a person, place or thing:

Person.

Sin is a master manipulator, a cunning deceiver, and a relentless destroyer. He's a parasite who feeds on human weakness, growing stronger with each compromise.

Imagine Alex, a successful businesswoman struggling with financial problems. Sin whispers, "You deserve more; take what's yours." At first, Alex resists, but Sin's persistent voice wears her down. She rationalizes, "It's just once; no one will notice." Sin seeps in, corrupting Alex's values and motivations.

It's crucial to remember that Sin is not who Alex is. Sin has dominion over Alex, corrupting and deceiving her. Alex, the person, is separate from the Sin that has taken hold.

Sin's grip on Alex has blinded her to consequences, justifies wrong actions, fuels greed and pride, destroys relationships, and separates her from God.

"For we do not wrestle against flesh and blood, but against the rulers, against the authorities, against the cosmic powers over this present darkness, against the spiritual forces of evil in the heavenly places." (Ephesians 6:12, ESV)

Place

The Kingdom of Sin is like a dark place., where the streets are paved with temptation, and the skyscrapers are built on lies. In this kingdom, the air reeks of corruption, and the water is poisoned with deceit. The kingdom of Sin is a place where we're lured by promises of power, pleasure, and control but ultimately find ourselves lost and enslaved.

According to Scripture, the Kingdom of Sin is a realm under the dominion of Satan, characterized by darkness, deception, slavery, separation from God, and corruption.

The Bible describes this kingdom as a sphere of influence where sin reigns, encompassing institutions, individuals, and spiritual forces.

In 1 John 2:15-17, we read, "Do not love the world or the things In the world. If anyone loves the world, the love of the Father is not in him. For all that is in the world—the desires of the flesh and the desires of the eyes and pride of life—is not from the Father but from the world."

In Romans 6:16-20, we see how individuals can become instruments of darkness: "Do you not know that if you present yourselves to anyone as obedient slaves, you are slaves of the one whom you obey, either of sin, which leads to death, or of obedience, which leads to righteousness? But thanks be to God that you who were once slaves of sin have become obedient from the heart to the standard of teaching to which you were committed."

Spiritual forces also play a significant role in this kingdom. Remember, Ephesians 6:12 states, "For we do not wrestle against flesh and blood, but against the rulers, against the authorities, against the cosmic powers over this present darkness, against the spiritual forces of evil in the heavenly places."

The Kingdom of Sin operates subtly, infiltrating our daily lives with distinct characteristics. Autonomy is a key feature, where sin seeks self-rule and opposes God's authority. We see this in everyday actions, such as taking credit for others' work or ideas, gossiping about coworkers or neighbors, or ignoring traffic laws and rules because "it won't hurt anyone." These seemingly minor infractions can establish a pattern of self-centeredness.

Another hallmark of the Kingdom of Sin is corruption, distorting creation and destroying its original intent. This manifests in wasteful habits like lazily consuming resources (water, electricity, paper), presenting a curated fake image on social media, or supporting exploitative labor practices through consumer choices. These actions may seem insignificant, but contribute to a broader culture of disregard.

Deception is another fundamental aspect, masquerading as truth and deceiving humanity. We engage in deception when downplaying harmful habits, exaggerating accomplishments or skills on resumes, or spreading unsubstantiated rumors or misinformation. These subtle distortions can become ingrained, leading us further from the truth.

The Kingdom of Sin seeks domination, enslaving individuals and separating them from God. This is evident in obsessive social media use, controlling thoughts and emotions, enabling or participating in addictive behaviors, or prioritizing material possessions over relationships or well-being.

Living in the Kingdom of Sin has dire consequences that affect our relationship with God and our spiritual well-being.

If you haven't noticed a common theme by now, you're not paying attention. One of the most significant consequences of sin is separation from God.

As Isaiah 59:2 states, "But your iniquities have made a separation between you and your God, and your sins have hidden his face from you so that he does not hear." This separation disrupts our connection with God, hindering our ability to receive guidance, comfort, and redemption.

Another devastating consequence is spiritual death. Ephesians

2:1-3 describes this state: "And you were dead in the trespasses and sins in which you once walked, following the course of this world, following the prince of the power of the air, the spirit that is now at work in the sons of disobedience." Spiritual death leaves us devoid of God's life-giving presence, making us vulnerable to sin's destructive power.

Ultimately, the final consequence of living in the Kingdom of Sin is destruction. Galatians 6:8 warns, "For the one who sows to his own flesh will from the flesh reap corruption, but the one who sows to the Spirit will from the Spirit reap eternal life." This destruction encompasses not only our spiritual lives but also our relationships, character, and eternal destiny.

These consequences underscore the urgency of recognizing and escaping the Kingdom of Sin.

Sin is a contagious and deadly pathogen, spreading through our choices and actions. This destructive force infects our hearts, minds, and relationships, causing devastation. It mutates and adapts, making detection and eradication challenging. However, its symptoms are unmistakable: guilt, shame, fear, and separation from others and ourselves.

Again, personifying Sin helps us grasp its profound impact on our lives. Imagine Sin as a cunning hacker, infiltrating and reprogramming our thoughts and desires, manipulating us to conform to its destructive agenda. Think about Sin as a dark kingdom, ruling with deception and oppression, enslaving us in its realm of darkness. Or picture Sin as a deadly virus, infecting and destroying our relationships, identity, and very essence.

Beloved, I am trying to show you sin's true nature; it is a malevolent force seeking domination and destruction.

Sin is not merely a theoretical concept or a laundry list of wrongdoings; it's an active enemy of our well-being, relentlessly working to undermine our potential. This force manipulates and deceives, leading us down a path of destruction.

As we explore the concept of Sin, it becomes clear that it's more than just any old noun – it's a destructive force that manifests in our lives and society. Sin perpetuates suffering and injustice, creating an environment where harm and exploitation thrive. Its influence seeps into every aspect of our existence, corrupting our relationships, distorting our identity, and separating us from our true potential.

Beloved, sin is a noun, and it is the enemy.

But wait, there's more.. sin is a verb, too.

Chapter 7
Sin As A Verb
An Action Or Choice.

To fully grasp the complexity of sin, we must also consider it as a verb. Sin is not just a condition or state but also an action that unfolds in the present moment.

It's a dynamic process that plays out in our lives, influenced by our decisions and choices. By considering sin as a verb, we can explore how it manifests in our daily actions, how it's reproduced and perpetuated, and how we can take steps to stop it and transform it. In the next section, we'll explore sin as a verb and how understanding it can lead us to a path of transformation and growth.

When "sin" is used as a verb, it describes how we are actively rebelling against God's design for our lives. We're choosing to go our own way rather than following His path. It's a deliberate act of disobedience, a choice to prioritize our own desires above God's will.

Imagine a master artist carefully crafting a beautiful work of art. But then, someone comes along and deliberately vandalizes it, destroying the beauty and intent of the original creation. That's what we do when we sin – we vandalize our own lives and the lives of those around us.

With each choice, we're either aligning ourselves with God's will or we're rebelling against it. We're either cultivating love, kindness, and compassion, or we're sowing discord, hurt, and destruction. The choice is ours.

Understanding the distinction between sin as a noun and sin as a verb helps us grasp the spiritual nature of sin, both as a state we are in and as choices that we make.

Recent studies reveal a troubling trend in how people perceive sin. A Barna Group survey found that only 35% of adults consider sin a significant issue in their lives (Barna Group, 2020). This staggering statistic indicates that nearly two-thirds of adults overlook or downplay the gravity of sin.

Further research by the Pew Research Center sheds light on the underlying attitudes. A striking 58% of Americans view sin as merely a moral failing, while 36% see it as a personal choice (Pew Research Center, 2019). This perspective reduces sin to a minor infraction or individual preference rather than recognizing its profound spiritual implications.

These findings suggest a widespread lack of understanding about sin's nature and consequences. Only about one-third of adults grasp the significance of sin, while the majority underestimate its impact. This limited awareness hinders individuals from confronting and overcoming sin, leaving them vulnerable to its destructive power.

As we delve deeper into the Kingdom of Sin, important questions arise. How does sin affect our relationships with God and others? Can we overcome sin through self-effort, or do we need God's help?

THE SIN DECEPTION

What's the difference between sin and mistakes? How does sin impact our daily choices and decisions?

Sin is often misunderstood or oversimplified. Merriam-Webster's Theological Dictionary defines sin as:

1. Violation of God's will or divine law.
2. Estrangement from God due to human disobedience.
3. Human nature is characterized by alienation from God and a propensity to evil.

Beloved, sin is a noun and a verb. Sin is a kingdom bent on your destruction. All very, very true. What is also true and the most important thing that you must learn is that sin is the orientation of your heart. Does your heart lean towards God and his kingdom, or is your heart bent towards the world and the kingdom of sin?

Beyond its definition as a noun, sin also functions as a verb – an action that separates us from God and others. To sin means to actively rebel against God's will, choosing self-interest over divine guidance. It involves intentionally disregarding moral boundaries, violating trust, and harming others. Sinning as an action perpetuates a cycle of disobedience, entangling us in its destructive power. Every sinful choice reinforces autonomy over submission, further estranging us from God's redeeming love. Recognizing sin as both a state and an action empowers us to confront its influence.

How does sin influence our lives? Does it lead to spiritual death, separation from God, or destructive habits? Can sin's consequences be reversed, or do they have lasting effects?

Can good works or behavior modification overcome sin? How

can we recognize and resist sin's influence in our daily lives?

How does sin impact our relationships, work, and community? Can people be held accountable for sin if they don't know better? What about "small" sins, like gossip or dishonesty – do they matter?

By exploring these questions and understanding sin's nature, we can better navigate its complex influence.

I recall a heartbreaking conversation with a dear friend struggling with addiction. His eyes were full of tears from the weight of shame and despair. He felt like a failure, trapped in a cycle he couldn't escape, and a disappointment to God, his family, and himself. Despite his best efforts, he couldn't break free.

His words echoed the Frustrations of many: "I try so hard, but I keep falling back into the same patterns. I feel like I'm letting everyone down, including God."

His struggle broke my heart. I've witnessed countless individuals grapple with similar feelings of inadequacy.

We've all faced moments where we feel like we're trying to measure up to an impossible standard, only to fall short. The weight of expectation, whether from ourselves or others, can crush our spirits. My friend's story reminded me of Paul's candid admission in Romans 7:15, "I do not understand what I do. For what I want to do, I do not do. And what I hate, I do."

The Apostle Paul, once a fierce persecutor of Christians, was transformed by God's grace. He endured immense suffering in prison for spreading the Gospel, yet continued teaching the truth about sin.

Paul's sufferings were extensive. He was imprisoned multiple times, beaten and whipped, stoned and left for dead, shipwrecked and stranded, and endured hunger, thirst and cold. Despite these hardships, his dedication to sharing God's word remained unwavering.

From his Roman prison cell, Paul penned powerful letters: Ephesians, emphasizing sin's destructive power; Philippians, encouraging faith amidst hardship; Colossians, exposing sin's roots in human nature; and Philemon, demonstrating forgiveness and redemption.

Paul had the Holy Spirit and the Gospel as revealed by Jesus. Paul had a clear and complete understanding of sin. He knew that the flesh was forever bent towards sin and that his primary task in life was to keep his heart focused on God. Paul did not have any money, he had no power, and he was in control of nothing. He didn't have a temple or a church; he had no audio system or light show, no mansion and no TV. Telethons.

Paul knew the truth that had been hidden from you.

Understanding the complexity of sin begins with one profoundly simple revelation.

Paul knows that sin begins when we take our eyes off of God.

His selfless dedication inspires us: "Whatever things were gained to me, those things I have counted as loss for the sake of Christ" (Philippians 3:7).

Paul's words underscore the complex, often baffling nature of sin. Even one of Christianity's most influential figures struggled with the disconnect between desire and action. This honest confession humanizes Paul and reminds us that our struggles aren't unique. We're not alone in this ongoing battle between flesh and spirit.

In Romans 7:25, Paul expresses gratitude for Jesus Christ, who delivers him from this inner turmoil. My friend's story, like Paul's, testifies to the power of god's grace.

This confession exposes the root of our struggle with sin. My friend's addiction isn't just a moral failing. It's not about him failing at all. His suffering is a symptom of a deeper issue. My friend is suffering from self-imposed separation from God. He has taken his eyes off of the Lord, who never fails and focused on the world and answers that never work. The Kingdom of Sin promises control, but this is a lie. We're deceived, justifying sinful choices and redefining good and evil to suit our desires.

Our attempts to self-medicate through habits like smoking, drinking, shopping, or casual sex only mask our pain temporarily, leading to more harm. These choices aim to manage pain and find escape but miss the underlying problem: rebellion against God's love and design.

Misunderstanding sin as a mere moral failing rather than fundamental rebellion against God hinders true freedom. We use the wrong measures, seeking self-sufficiency instead of surrendering to God's transformative power.

We see sin in simple terms and are completely unprepared to rule over it.

What is the real problem here?

Sin is not just about making mistakes or poor choices.

Remember, in the Bible, sin is described as a powerful force that seeks to dominate and destroy us. It's a spiritual disease that infects every part of our being, causing us to turn away from God and toward our own selfish desires.

The famous painter Caravaggio was a master of light and shadow. But his life was also marked by darkness and sin. He was known for his volatile temper, and in 1606, he killed a young man in a duel. Filled with guilt and remorse, Caravaggio fled Rome and spent the rest of his life on the run, always looking over his shoulder.

During this time, he painted some of his most famous works, including "David with the Head of Goliath" and "The Taking of Christ." In these paintings, he explored themes of sin, guilt, and redemption. He saw himself in the characters he painted, and his art became a way of processing his own struggles with sin.

You have to ask yourself, was Caravaggio running towards God or away from his sin? If the sin happened in Rome, how far must he run to escape? Do you see the problem? When our heart is not bent towards the Lord, it doesn't matter where we go, and sin still has dominion.

How many times have you seen people move and start over? How many times have you discovered that the problems always come, too?

You can't outrun your heart, and sin always starts there.

You can't run from sin, and more often than not, the kingdom of sin is bringing the world down around you.

The consequences of sin's dominion are far-reaching, contributing to some of humanity's darkest moments, including wars, genocides, oppression and injustice.

The Rwandan genocide, which occurred in 1994, is a devastating example of the impact of sin on society. Over the course of 100 days, an estimated 800,000 people, primarily from the Tutsi ethnic group, were killed by the Hutu majority. The roots of this tragedy can be traced back to the Belgian colonial era when the seeds of ethnic division and hatred were sown. Years of oppression, discrimination, and violence culminated in a horrific display of sin's destructive power. The genocide was fueled by sin's destructive forces, including pride and prejudice, fear and hatred, greed and power struggles.

The impact of sin was evident in the brutal killings and massacres and the destruction of communities and families. The Displacement and trauma of survivors added to the long-term effects on the nation's psyche and economy.

The kingdom of sin is a kingdom of destruction and death. This dark moment in human history is a stark reminder of the immeasurable impact of sin on society. It shows how sin can lead to unimaginable suffering, destruction, and chaos.

The effects of sin in society continue to manifest in various ways. The #MeToo movement has brought attention to the pervasive issue of sexual harassment and assault, revealing the profound impact of sin on human relationships and society.

Studies have shown that a significant portion of the population has experienced sexual violence, with one in three women and one in six men experiencing sexual violence in the United States alone (National Sexual Violence Resource Center, 2020). Additionally, research has indicated that the majority of sexual assaults go unreported (National Sexual Violence Resource Center, 2020).

The movement has also highlighted the stories of individuals who have experienced sexual harassment and assault, including high-profile figures who have shared their experiences and sparked a wider conversation about consent and power (Burke, 2018). The fallout from these revelations has been significant, with several high-profile figures facing consequences for their actions (The New York Times, 2018).

Beloved, stop for a minute and think about your life again. Has sexual violence had an impact on you or the people you love? Sexual Violence is an all too common problem in the kingdom of sin.

Research has also shown that the majority of Americans believe that sexual harassment and assault are major problems in society, indicating a growing awareness of the issue and a desire for change (Pew Research Center, 2020).

In a heartbreaking scene that has become all too familiar, a young mother lies motionless on the floor of her home, surrounded by toys and photos of her children. Her lifeless body is a testament to the devastating grip of opioid addiction, a crisis that has ravaged communities and stolen countless lives. But this tragedy is more than just a statistic or a headline – it is a stark reminder of the destructive power of sin, which has left a trail of shattered dreams, broken relationships, and unspeakable suffering in its wake.

The opioid crisis has underscored the destructive impact of sin on individuals and communities, resulting in widespread addiction, suffering, and loss. According to the National Institute on Drug Abuse (2020), over 2.5 million Americans struggle with opioid use disorder, with opioid-related overdoses claiming tens of thousands of lives annually.

Research has shown that opioid addiction is often linked to deeper issues, including mental health concerns, trauma, and social and economic factors (Koch et al., 2019). The crisis has also had a devastating impact on families and communities, with many experiencing loss and grief as a result of opioid-related deaths (Gomes et al., 2018).

Furthermore, the economic toll of the opioid crisis has been significant, with estimated costs exceeding $1 trillion since 2001 (Council of Economic Advisers, 2017). The crisis has also placed a burden on healthcare and social services, highlighting the need for comprehensive solutions and support.

Sin's devastating impact on humanity perpetuates cycles of harm and pain worldwide. It's more than a mistake or lapse in judgment; sin is a deliberate rebellion against God's authority, driven by selfish desires.

Again, to grasp sin's complexity, we must move beyond simplistic definitions. Sin separates us from God, exerting destructive power that causes immense suffering. This separation occurs when we prioritize our will over God's, disrupting our connection with Him.

Sin exercises profound dominance over humanity, manifesting in five key ways:

Sin corrupts our hearts, fueling desires that contradict God's will and distorts our thinking, clouding judgment and perception. It destroys relationships, fostering division and isolation, and enslaves us to harmful habits and desires. Ultimately, sin blocks spiritual growth, hindering intimacy with God and preventing us from experiencing His intended love, joy and freedom.

We are being held captive by a force separating us from our true home and Father's love. This is sin's reality – a state of separation dominating humanity. Again, sin prevents us from experiencing God's intended love, joy and freedom.

Let me share the true story of Eric Lomax, a British Army officer during World War II, who illustrates the dictatorial power of sin.

Beloved, ask yourself, What happens when anger, bitterness and despair rule your life? What happens when you focus on all the things wrong in the world and how unfairly you were treated?

Lomax was captured by the Japanese and sent to a POW camp, where he was subjected to brutal treatment and forced labor.

After the war, Lomax struggled with anger, bitterness, and hatred towards his captors, particularly one Japanese officer, Takashi Nagase. These emotions consumed him, distorting his thinking, corrupting his heart, and destroying his relationships.

Years later, Lomax discovered that Nagase was still alive and sought him out.

Do you know why he sought him out?

Why would YOU seek out the man who had imprisoned and tortured you?

I am sure some of you were not thinking about revenge. Well done.

The rest of us?

Well, that's why we where "what would Jesus do bracelets" to remind us of what Jesus would do. Just kidding,

I lost all mine.

Let me share Mr. Lomax's own words about the matter.

"Bitterness and anger had nearly consumed me… But gradually, incrementally, the corrosive effects of those emotions began to recede, replaced by a sense of calm, of acceptance."

Do you know what else he wrote in his book?

"I had been consumed by hatred, and it had nearly destroyed me."

"Forgiveness is not easy, but it is essential for healing."

"The past was still there, but it no longer controlled me."

"I realized that I had been given a second chance, and I was determined to make the most of it."

Instead of seeking revenge, Lomax chose to forgive Nagase, which began a journey of healing and redemption. Lomax's story illustrates how Sin's power can hold us captive, but God's love and forgiveness can set us free.

Lomax's story is told in his book, "The Railway Man," and was adapted into a film in 2013. It's a powerful example of how Sin's grip can be broken, and freedom, love, and joy can be restored through forgiveness and redemption.

It's time to expose another lie that binds: The past has power.

The concept of "the past has power" refers to the enduring impact of historical events, experiences and traumas on individuals, communities and societies. This idea acknowledges that past injustices, abuses and sufferings continue to influence present-day realities.

The past's influence shapes our understanding of ourselves and the world around us. Historical experiences have a lasting impact on cultural identity, informing values, beliefs and worldviews. These experiences create narratives that inform current perspectives and attitudes.

All of that is completely true.

However, the idea is that unaddressed traumas and injustices define you; your past determines your future. It is a lie from the kingdom of sin.

The world has fallen, and people are being harmed, exploited and oppressed. This often leads to feelings of powerlessness, trauma and stigma. Powerlessness manifests as a loss of control and agency, while trauma leaves emotional and psychological scars. Stigma attaches social shame and marginalization to the victim.

Victimhood can lead to a victim mentality, focusing on past injustices and perpetuating helplessness.

The past, though significant, does not dictate our present or future. We should acknowledge and learn from history, but we are not defined by it. Our experiences, whether painful or triumphant, do not determine our worth or identity.

There's a disconnect in how we perceive the past's influence. We emphasize that our past actions don't define us, yet societal narratives often assert that what happened to us shapes who we are. This inconsistency breeds doubt, shame and guilt.

God's perspective clarifies our true identity. He defines us, not our experiences or choices. Sin seeks to distort this truth, tempting us to accept a flawed definition of ourselves.

Embracing God's definition frees us from the weight of past hurts and mistakes. It empowers us to rise above societal expectations and forge a path guided by divine purpose.

Chapter 8
The Kingdom of Sin

The kingdom of sin wields profound influence over every aspect of human existence, including our thoughts, emotions, and actions. This realm of darkness severs our relationship with God, leaving us reliant on our own strength and perpetuating spiritual death. The kingdom of sin spreads ignorance, confusion, and misinformation, akin to being trapped in a fake news echo chamber where truth is distorted.

This toxic environment fuels misconceptions and misunderstandings, making it impossible to discern truth from lies. The COVID-19 pandemic exemplifies the dangers of such echo chambers, where misinformation and disinformation lead to harmful decisions and real-world consequences. Similarly, the kingdom of sin expertly programs us to prioritize self-rule, subtly influencing our thoughts, desires, and actions.

This insidious programming often masquerades as free will, manipulating our choices and actions. It begins with the lies and half-truths we absorb from media, culture, and personal experiences, shaping our perceptions, desires, and values. As we internalize these messages, they become ingrained thought patterns, driving our decisions. For instance, constant exposure to sensual imagery programs our minds to crave more, leading to lust and unhealthy desires.

The kingdom of sin crafts a script that we unknowingly follow, tempting us with promises of satisfaction or escape.

Again, remember the apostle Paul writes in Romans *7:14-15 (ESV),* "For we know that the law is spiritual, but I am of the flesh, sold under sin, for I do not understand my own actions. For I do not do what I want, but I do the very thing I hate." Paul's words reveal the struggle we all face: our choices are often driven by the programming of Sin rather than our true desires or values.

The kingdom of Sin has a profound impact on our thoughts, desires, and actions, often leading us to make choices that align with its agenda. We may believe we're making conscious decisions, but in reality, we're frequently responding to the programming of Sin.

Consider the temptation to gossip. Did you really want to engage in gossip, or was it the influence of media and culture, such as "Gossip Girls" and "Spill the Tea," that programmed you to crave the latest scoop? These messages shape our perceptions and desires, making us more susceptible to Sin's influence.

Beloved, what about that? Does the media you are consuming affect what you think? Think back. Have you ever seen a post or a TikTok video that caused you to get mad or feel offended? Ever seen a post that you ad to share to raise awareness? Have you ever watched a political ad and felt frustration or anger?

Come on, we have all seen the iconic ASPCA commercial featuring Sarah McLachlan's emotional ballad "Angel." The ad showcases heartbreaking images of abused and neglected animals, with McLachlan's haunting voiceover.

If you have seen it, you know it's a tear-jerker, and its message worked. People were programmed to donate, and they responded wonderfully. I happen to like dogs and cats.

Ask yourself, what is being programmed in your life?

Similarly, when it comes to substance abuse, did you truly want that hit, or was it the kingdom of Sin's lie that told you you needed it to cope or feel good? Did sin whisper that no one will know and without it you will be nervous and awkward? Has sin been telling you for weeks that it's not the problem, that it helps you think better?

The pressure to conform to societal norms or escape emotional pain can be overwhelming, leading us to make choices that harm ourselves and others.

Even our emotions, like anger and frustration, can be influenced by the kingdom of Sin. Did you want to lose your temper, or has the kingdom of Sin been pressuring you all day, whispering lies and fueling your irritation?

Think about that for a moment. Did you know that these are the 5 reasons people gave for exploding into road rage?

The insignificant factors that trigger road rage:

1. Minor traffic infractions (e.g., accidental cutting off)

Keep in mind that these factors are subjective and may vary in significance from person to person.

Seriously though, people are ready to throw hands or shoot someone over being cut off in traffic. What is happening in the world?

The constant bombardment of stress, anxiety, and negativity can wear us down, making us more prone to outbursts and sinful behavior.

These examples illustrate the power Sin has over us, often operating beneath our conscious awareness. It's essential to recognize this influence, not to excuse our choices, but to understand the depth of Sin's grip on our lives.

The human mind is akin to a computer, susceptible to programming by external influences. Media and marketing are the master coders, weaving a narrative that shapes our desires, preferences, and behaviors. Through subtle yet powerful techniques, they create a programming language that influences our perceptions, dictating what we think, feel, and do.

Children are particularly vulnerable to this programming. Toy advertising, for instance, creates a desire for material possessions, often leading to tantrums and demands. Sugary cereal marketing uses colorful packaging and cartoon characters to make unhealthy choices appealing, programming lifelong preferences for sugary foods. Social media influencers present curated, idealized content, fostering unrealistic expectations and desires that can lead to body dissatisfaction, low self-esteem, and consumerism.

As we grow older, this programming continues, often operating beneath our conscious awareness. We become conditioned to respond to certain cues, making choices that align with the narrative created by media and marketing.

The echo chambers of Sin played a significant role in the tragedy that is the COVID-19 pandemic. By sowing confusion, mistrust, and division, they created an environment where truth was a casualty. People were more likely to listen to those who confirmed their biases than to credible sources. The result was a pandemic of misinformation with devastating consequences.

As we breathe in this toxic air, we become increasingly divided, strife-ridden, and lost. The kingdom of sin manipulates and controls us, using our own thoughts and emotions against us.

Again, the opioid epidemic is a heart-wrenching example of the kingdom of sin's manipulative power. Sin takes hold of our legitimate pain and emotions, whispering lies that a pill will bring relief and happiness. As we succumb, it gradually controls our thoughts and actions, fueling addiction and destroying lives.

Consider the true story of Patrick Kennedy, son of Senator Ted Kennedy, who struggled with addiction for decades. He thought opioid medication would alleviate his physical and emotional pain but soon found himself trapped in a cycle of addiction, losing his career, relationships, and nearly his life.

But Patrick found redemption through God's love and grace. With treatment and support, he broke free from Sin's grasp, finding healing, restoration, and true freedom from addiction. Today, he advocates for mental health and addiction support, helping others escape the kingdom of sin's deadly grip.

Patrick's story illustrates how the kingdom of sin exploits our vulnerabilities, using our own thoughts and emotions against us.

The kingdom of sin blinds us to the truth, causing us to wander in a world of relativism and moral ambiguity.

For instance, a person struggling with addiction may know the devastating consequences of their actions yet continue to engage in self-destructive behavior.

How many times have you heard the excuses…. They are all basically the same.

Why you will Definitely, absolutely, for yourself this time, quit……………

Tomorrow.

Zachery Tims was a prominent youth pastor and author known for his charismatic ministry and outreach to young people. However, behind the scenes, Tims struggled with addiction and hidden sin. He became entangled in a web of moral ambiguity, where he justified his actions and ignored the warning signs of his destructive behavior.

Despite his success and popularity, Tim's life began to unravel. His addiction and secrets took a devastating toll on his relationships, ministry, and, ultimately, his life. In 2011, Tims was found dead in a New York City hotel room, a victim of his own struggles with sin and addiction.

Tim's story serves as a powerful reminder of the kingdom of sin's blinding power. His life illustrates how easily we can become trapped in a world of moral relativism, where right and wrong become distorted. His tragic end also highlights the Importance of seeking help, accountability, and redemption.

Tim's legacy now serves as a cautionary tale, urging others to confront their own struggles with sin and addiction. His story encourages us to seek truth, forgiveness, and restoration in God's love and grace rather than becoming entangled in the kingdom of sin's deadly grip.

The kingdom of sin also perpetuates bondage, which manifests as slavery to our sinful desires and habits. We become prisoners of our own making, trapped in cycles of sin and shame. A person struggling with pornography may feel trapped and powerless to stop despite their best efforts.

The story of Josh McDowell, a well-known Christian author and speaker, illustrates the kingdom of sin's perpetuation of bondage. McDowell has publicly shared his personal struggle with pornography addiction, which began at age eight and continued for over 20 years.

McDowell describes feeling trapped and powerless to stop despite his best efforts. He was a prisoner of his own making, stuck in a cycle of sin and shame. However, through God's grace and redemption, McDowell found freedom from his addiction.

McDowell's story highlights the kingdom of sin's ability to enslave us to our sinful desires and habits. He thought he was alone in his struggle but found that millions of others were similarly trapped. Today, McDowell openly shares his testimony to help others break free from the bondage of sin.

Beloved, he took his eyes off of God and focused on lust and fell to sin. He took his eyes off the world and focused on God and was restored. It wasn't the program; it wasn't the confessional and penitents. It wasn't his willpower or even the dedication of his sponsor. Sure, all of those things can help, but the only answer to sin is God.

The kingdom of sin can masquerade as depression, whispering lies of hopelessness and despair. But what if the true enemy is not our emotions or mental state but the kingdom of sin itself? One more time, remember Paul writes, "For we do not wrestle against flesh and blood, but against the rulers, against the authorities, against the cosmic powers over this present darkness, against the spiritual forces of evil in the heavenly places." *(Ephesians 6:12, ESV).*

At its core, the kingdom of sin perpetuates separation from God and isolation from others. This disconnection is the root of all sin, including addiction and depression. When we're separated from God, we're severed from the source of life, hope, and joy.

As David lamented, "I am poured out like water, and all my bones are out of joint; my heart is like wax; it is melted within my breast" *(Psalm 22:14, ESV).*

Being separated from God is depressing. It's a state of spiritual darkness where we're left to face our struggles alone.

Addiction and depression are symptoms of this deeper issue – a cry for connection, for meaning, for life. They're attempts to fill the void left by our separation from God. But only God can truly satisfy our deepest longings. As Augustine wrote, "You have made us for yourself, O Lord and our hearts are restless until they rest in you."

The heart-wrenching story of Amy Bleuel, founder of Project Semicolon, exemplifies the kingdom of sin's devastating impact. Amy struggled with depression, anxiety, and suicidal thoughts, feeling abandoned and isolated from God and others. She described her journey as walking through a dark valley, alone and without hope.

Despite her efforts to find solace, Amy felt disconnected from God's love and grace. The kingdom of sin perpetuated her sense of separation, leading to intense loneliness and despair. However, in her darkest moments, Amy found glimmers of hope. She began to share her story, connecting with others who struggled similarly.

Through her journey, Amy discovered that she was not alone. She found community, support, and, ultimately, redemption. Amy's story highlights the kingdom of sin's ability to perpetuate separation from God, but also the power of connection, hope, and redemption. Tragically, Amy passed away in 2017, but her legacy lives on through Project Semicolon, which continues to support those struggling with mental health issues.

The kingdom of sin has far-reaching effects on humanity, causing us to live in a state of spiritual death and separation from God.

There are few examples of the evil in the world worse than Human Trafficking.

Cyntoia Brown's heart-wrenching story lays bare the horrific realities of sex trafficking in the United States. At just 16 years old, Cyntoia was ensnared by a ruthless pimp and forced into prostitution, subjected to relentless rape, beatings, and exploitation. Her trafficker controlled every aspect of her life, crushing her spirit and stealing her innocence.

In a desperate bid for survival, Cyntoia killed a man who had paid to rape her. Yet, despite the unimaginable trauma she endured, she was tried as an adult and condemned to life in prison.

Does that story bother you? Are you asking yourself, how could this happen? She is the victim, right?

Of course, you are right. What you should really be asking yourself is why does the government have the power to stop COVID misinformation and Jihad propaganda but not child pornography and sex trafficking sites?

Who is using these services?

Ask yourself?

Who are the individuals participating in these high-profile events and private gatherings?

Specifically, who are the guests attending lavish parties at Epstein's Island and Diddy's exclusive soirees?

Are they influential business leaders, celebrities, politicians, or other powerful figures?

Are they speaking into your life and the life of your children?

The outcry that followed Cyntoia's conviction shed light on the systemic failures that enable sex trafficking to thrive. The grooming and manipulation of vulnerable youth, the exploitation of those most in need of protection, and the glaring lack of support for trafficking victims all contributed to Cyntoia's nightmare.

THE SIN DECEPTION

Cyntoia's story became a catalyst for change. After serving 15 long years, she was granted clemency and released from prison in 2019. Her journey underscores the urgent need for increased awareness and education, stronger laws safeguarding victims, and comprehensive support services for survivors. We must confront the kingdom of sin's destructive power and advocate for justice.

Cyntoia's case serves as a powerful reminder that we must do better. We must create a society where vulnerable youth are shielded from exploitation, where victims receive compassion and support, and where perpetrators face justice. As people of faith, we are called to defend the weak, uphold the cause of the poor, and seek justice.

The kingdom of sin is a powerful force that shapes our lives and world in ways we often overlook. The Bible warns us that sin has dominion, and we must not underestimate its influence. This kingdom has a structure, hierarchy, and reach, shaping our thoughts, actions, and relationships in harmful ways. At its core is a system of thought patterns, behaviors, and relationships that perpetuate sin, trapping us in a cycle of self-destruction.

Think about a person struggling with addiction again. Alcohol or drug abuse often starts as a coping mechanism or a means to fit in, but it quickly becomes a master that controls and destroys lives. Remember, it is the kingdom of sin whispering lies, "You need me to feel good," or "You can't function without me." Before long, the addict is trapped in a vicious cycle, unable to break free from the grip of sin. This is the kingdom of sin at work, perpetuating destructive patterns and thoughts and leading us further away from God's design for our lives.

This vicious cycle constantly reinforces our worst impulses and tendencies, making it nearly impossible to break free without God's intervention.

The kingdom of sin is a formidable foe; we must recognize the kingdom of sin's influence in the world. The kingdom of sin uses a system that perpetuates sin by promoting a thought pattern that values self-interest over others. This insidious mindset prioritizes individual success and happiness above all else, leading to a self-centered and narcissistic culture.

The Enron scandal, which led to the company's bankruptcy in 2001, is a stark example of the kingdom of sin's influence in the world. Enron's corporate culture embodied the kingdom of sin's values, prioritizing self-interest and profit over ethics and accountability.

Executives like Jeffrey Skilling and Kenneth Lay fostered a mindset that valued individual success and wealth above all else, leading to a culture of greed, deception, and exploitation. This self-centered approach resulted in catastrophic consequences, including the loss of thousands of jobs, billions of dollars in investor losses, and a damaged economy.

The Enron scandal illustrates how the kingdom of sin's influence can permeate even the highest levels of society, leading to a narcissistic culture that prioritizes power and wealth over people and principles.

In the kingdom of Sin, people become isolated and disconnected, using technology and social media as a substitute for genuine human interaction. This fosters a culture of disconnection, where relationships are superficial and transactional rather than deep and meaningful. Even in the midst of a crowded community, people may feel lonely and disconnected.

This culture of disconnection perpetuates sin by reinforcing the idea that we are alone and that our actions do not impact others. The kingdom of sin also perpetuates its influence through a system that creates a sense of competition and scarcity, where individuals feel pitted against each other for resources and success. For instance, consider the cutthroat culture of corporate ladder climbing, where colleagues become adversaries, and success is measured by who can step on the most rungs. This system encourages a culture of consumerism and materialism, where happiness and fulfillment are measured by what we own and what we achieve. Think about the endless stream of advertisements telling us we need the latest gadget or fashion trend to be happy.

Think about how easy it is to Envy others. Look at what they have. He is only 25 and already bought a house. She is 22 and already has a family. He is rich and must have had rich parents. This car, that bag, this kind of make-up, that kind of shoes, and let's not even start on the latest phones.

This system also fosters a sense of shame and guilt, where individuals feel unworthy and unlovable if they don't have X. Worse still, this kind of comparison creates a world where their mistakes and failures are met with judgment and condemnation. *Your brother got straight A's. What's wrong with you? Your sister moved out when she was 18. Why can't you get a job?*

Comparison kills gratitude, and most of the time, it results in bullying.

Consider the devastating impact of cyberbullying, where young people are mercilessly mocked and shamed online. Overall, this system perpetuates sin by promoting a self-centered and isolationist mindset, which leads to a culture of disconnection and perpetuates harmful behaviors and relationships.

The hierarchy of the dominion of sin is equally insidious, prioritizing self-interest and short-term gains over long-term consequences and ethical considerations.

It's like a game of musical chairs, where everyone is fighting for the last seat, regardless of who gets hurt. This hierarchy is deeply ingrained in our culture and our own hearts, leading us to compromise our values and principles for the sake of convenience or pleasure.

Within the realms of business, media and society, influential figures dominate the landscape. These individuals, often driven by ambition and self-interest, may unknowingly serve the kingdom of sin or actively promote its agenda.

Some are unwitting pawns manipulated by the subtle forces of sin. They prioritize power, wealth and status over moral principles, perpetuating a cycle of corruption.

Others are deliberate operatives and ambassadors, actively advancing the kingdom of sin. They strategically shape public opinion, policies and cultural narratives to align with sinful values.

A sobering truth is many people willingly serve sin, often

unaware of its destructive consequences. This pervasive allegiance undermines collective well-being, fostering a culture of self-centeredness and moral decay.

Social media platforms, in particular, are leveraged by the kingdom of sin to perpetuate its purposes. They are designed to keep us scrolling, enslaving many people for extended periods. The kingdom of sin exploits these platforms to structure our attention and behavior around likes, shares, and followers, hierarchizing our self-worth and identity based on online validation.

Curated and manipulated content influences our relationships and mental health, often perpetuating unrealistic beauty standards and materialistic values. The kingdom of sin uses social media's design to its advantage, shaping our choices and actions in ways that align with its purposes.

In this sense, the kingdom of sin is not just a passive state of separation from God but an active and intelligent force that seeks to shape our culture and individual lives in ways that oppose God's design.

The Kingdom of Sin is a force of expansion and darkness, seeking to ensnare people in its grasp. Characterized by spiritual blindness, it's a realm of bondage where desires, fears and addictions hold people captive. Sin expands through fragmentation, isolation and despair, disconnecting individuals from God, themselves and others.

This cycle is illustrated by the story of Brian Welch, former Korn lead guitarist, and his experience as he struggled with depression and addiction.

Beloved, have you ever been depressed? Not sad, but depressed as a state of being? Exhausted, stressed out and ready to stay in bed for a week? Ever felt alone, even in the middle of a crowd?

This is what is happening to Brian. He is amazing and popular, and people are around Brian all the time.

His encounter with God's kingdom transformed his life. Surrendering to Christ, Brian reconnected with God, himself and others, overcoming depression and addiction. Now, he shares his story to free others from sin's grip.

Again, The Kingdom of Sin exploits vulnerabilities, perpetuating harmful norms through platforms like social media, shaping choices aligning with its purposes.

The kingdom of sin has launched a devastating attack on our children, sexualizing them at an alarming rate and corrupting their innocence. This is a clear manifestation of the kingdom's intent to destroy God's creation and enslave humanity.

By targeting vulnerable young minds, the kingdom of sin has created a culture where children are encouraged to explore and express their sexuality at an age when they are not emotionally or psychologically equipped to handle it. This has led to a distorted view of identity, where a person is primarily defined by their sexual orientation or gender identity rather than their inherent value and worth as a child of God.

The kingdom of sin has infiltrated every aspect of our children's lives, from sexual education that focuses on pleasure and exploration rather than values and boundaries to social media platforms that expose them to explicit content and influencer culture. Gender ideology tells children they can choose their gender and pronouns, and entertainment and media sexualize children and normalize their exposure to adult themes.

This is a deliberate attempt by the kingdom of sin to corrupt childhood innocence, create confusion and uncertainty, normalize sexual experimentation, and enslave children to their desires and fears.

Beloved, are you going to stand idly by while our children are exploited and harmed? Think about your life and the world you live in. Either you are on the side of children, or you are on the side of exploitation.

We must recognize the kingdom of sin's tactics and stand against this sexualization of children. We must protect and empower them with truth, values, and a biblical worldview that honors God's design and purpose for their lives.

We must declare that children are precious and worthy of protection and that their innocence and childhood should be preserved and cherished. We must educate them with wisdom and values and shield them from the harmful influences of the kingdom of sin. We must pray for them and with them and ask God to guard their hearts and minds.

Together, we can create a safe and nurturing environment where children can grow and thrive, free from the corrupting influence of the kingdom of sin.

As soon as I wrote that, I knew it wasn't true…

But we can try. We can give it our best shot.

Don't you think they are worth it?

In this sense, sin is not just an action or a behavior; it is a state of being, a power that reigns, and a dominion that holds humanity captive. It is a kingdom that operates in the world, manifesting as darkness, bondage, and separation from God.

It's time we learned more about Sin, not as the kingdom with dominion but as a choice, action, a verb.

In ***Genesis 39:9 ESV***,

"No one is greater in this house than I am, and he has withheld nothing from me except you because you are his wife. How then can I do this great wickedness and sin against God?"

 Here, we find the first use of the word "sin" as a verb.

Joseph asked how he could "do" such a great wickedness, recognizing how his action would be a sin. How his choice to participate in such wickedness would be a sin against God.

A pivotal moment in the biblical narrative occurs when Joseph faces temptation and grapples with sinning against God. To understand this moment, let's recap Joseph's story. As the favorite son of Jacob, Joseph received a special gift – a beautiful coat – which sparked jealousy in his brothers. They plotted against him and sold him into slavery. However, in the household of Potiphar, an Egyptian official, Joseph thrived due to his wisdom, administrative skills, and God's blessing.

As his responsibilities grew, so did the attention from Potiphar's wife. She attempted to seduce Joseph, but he refused, recognizing that giving in would betray Potiphar's trust and, more importantly, be a sin against God. Despite her persistence, Joseph stood firm, declaring, "How then can I do this great wickedness and sin against God?" *(Genesis 39:9).*

This moment marked a critical turning point in Joseph's journey as well, demonstrating his unwavering commitment to his faith and his refusal to compromise his values, even in the face of temptation.

"No one is greater in this house than I am. He has withheld nothing from me except you because you are his wife. How then can I do this great wrong and sin against God?" *(Genesis 39:9, ESV)*

Joseph recognizes that sinning against Potiphar's wife would ultimately be a sin against God Himself. This understanding reflects the biblical concept of sin as a rebellion against God's authority and design.

As Matthew Henry notes in his commentary, "Joseph views this sin as a violation of God's law and an offense against His sovereignty." *(Henry, 1994)*

John Calvin similarly observes, "Joseph's words imply that he regarded sin as a violation of God's will, and a breach of His commandments." *(Calvin, 1842)*

A pervasive notion exists that to truly make amends, we must go to those we've wronged and make restitution. This mindset perpetuates a transactional view of forgiveness: "Do wrong, do right, all better."

It's time to expose another lie that binds.

Have you ever heard the tenant say that in order to stay sober, you have to go to all the people you wronged while drunk and make amends?

Have you ever heard that if you wronged someone, you have to make it right?

We see this in various contexts, such as making amends to others as a condition for forgiveness, parents requiring children to work off debts for mistakes, confessing to clergy and offering payment for absolution.

We think like that. Do wrong, make right

I did wrong, I do right, all better.

All is forgiven. It's water under the bridge.

Still need more forgiveness, go to the priest and confess maybe even drop a few coins in the box. All good now, right?

Very transactional.

That is what the world and the church want us to believe.

That is the lie that binds us!

Sin is always an offense against God. It starts with a heart bent towards self and always ends in sin against God.

The world and the church reduce forgiveness to a simple exchange, overlooking a crucial truth. Sin is always an offense against God, stemming from a self-centered heart. Forgiveness isn't solely about human reconciliation but about divine reconciliation. While making restitution is important, it's insufficient for true forgiveness. Only God can forgive sins.

How many times have you said sorry, tried to make it right and still felt guilty? Beloved, when we sin, we hide from God; we separate ourselves. Nothing we do on earth can fix that separation. We feel guilt and shame for years after having made a mends. Some people try and make a mend only to spend a lifetime wallowing in guilt and shame.

You can be forgiven by the people you have wronged but only God can forgive you of your sin.

Should you do all those things? Make it right, and pay for your mistakes… of course, you can not be forgiven, not truly forgiven, until you ask God to forgive you. And even then… God is just, and sin must be paid for.

God's forgiveness isn't transactional; it's rooted in His justice and mercy. Sin's consequences must be addressed, but God's forgiveness is available through genuine repentance.

This understanding of sin as a rebellious heart towards God's authority is echoed in the words of Augustine, who writes, "Sin is a turning away from God, and a turning towards oneself." *(Augustine, 397)*

Sin is also a deliberate and intentional act, a conscious choice to disobey God's will and character. It's a dynamic and purposeful decision to reject God's design, manifesting in various ways.

The story of Bernard Madoff, the mastermind behind the largest Ponzi scheme in history, exemplifies sin as a deliberate and intentional act. Madoff's decision to deceive and manipulate thousands of investors, causing financial ruin and emotional distress, was a conscious choice to reject God's design.

Madoff's actions demonstrate a refusal to trust in God's goodness and sovereignty, instead relying on his own cunning and deceit to achieve success. His sin was not just a mistake or a lapse in judgment but a purposeful decision to prioritize his own interests over the well-being of others.

Madoff's intentional disobedience to God's will and character led to a life of secrecy, anxiety, and, ultimately, destruction. His story serves as a stark reminder that sin is a deliberate choice with devastating consequences.

Sin's insidious nature is often revealed in our violation of God's commands and principles. David's infamous adultery and cover-up serve as a poignant reminder. As Israel's king, David was entrusted with modeling integrity, but instead, he succumbed to sin's allure.

David's downward spiral began with an illicit affair with Bathsheba, a married woman, directly violating God's command against adultery. Desperate to conceal his transgression, David orchestrated the brutal murder of Bathsheba's husband, Uriah, flagrantly disregarding God's command against murder. David's web of deceit ensnared others as he manipulated and lied to those around him.

God sent Nathan, the prophet, to call out David. Nathan's

message was clear and direct, confronting David about his grave sin.

Nathan accused David of several things,

Murdering Uriah the Hittite

Taking Bathsheba, Uriah's wife, for himself

Disregarding God's laws and commandments

Showing no compassion or justice to Uriah

Bringing shame and dishonor to God's name

Nathan's bold confrontation forced David to confront the severity of his sins, sparking a turning point in his journey.

David's story demonstrates sin's destructive power, damaging relationships, tarnishing his reputation and threatening his kingdom's stability. His experience serves as a stark reminder that our choices have lasting consequences, affecting not only ourselves but also those around us.

Pause again, beloved. Think about your life and the world you live in. Do you know a family that has been destroyed by adultery, abandonment and sin?

Sin is just as destructive today as it was for King David.

Beloved, sin is almost always a matter of prioritizing one's own desires above God's will.

We've all been there – faced with a choice between following our own desires or following God's will. It's easy to get caught up in the idea that our own way is the best way and that God's plan is restrictive or outdated. But the truth is, when we prioritize our own desires above

God's will, we're choosing to rebel against His character and commands.

This can play out in subtle ways, like choosing to cheat on a test or exaggerating the truth to get ahead. Or it can manifest in more significant ways, like prioritizing our own ambitions over the well-being of others. Whatever the case, sin is an active choice – a deliberate act of rebellion against God.

When we choose to go our own way, we're not just making a passive mistake – we're actively rejecting God's guidance and wisdom. And the consequences can be severe, leading to separation, suffering, and darkness.

Elizabeth Holmes, the founder of Theranos, ignored God's wisdom and the expertise of the people around her. Pursuing success at any cost. Driven by ambition and greed, she cheated investors, patients and partners through deception and fraud.

Her dishonesty started with small deceptions but escalated into catastrophic harm. Initially, she forged test results and falsified data, misrepresenting Theranos' technology capabilities. She faked demonstrations and product trials, concealing failures and setbacks. As time passed, her actions became more egregious, manipulating employees and intimidating whistleblowers.

Holmes also misused funds and resources, putting patients' lives at risk with inaccurate test results. Theranos' collapse serves as a stark reminder of sin's destructive power. Holmes' story echoes biblical warnings about deceit, pride and disregard for truth. Her tragic fall highlights the universal struggle with sin, underscoring the importance of humility, accountability and seeking God's wisdom.

Sin tempts us all, regardless of position or background, to disregard God's guidance. We see it in business leaders prioritizing profits over people, individuals engaging in reckless behavior, and communities turning a blind eye to injustice. These actions have far-reaching consequences, causing harm and destruction.

The parallel between Holmes' story and the foolish builder in Matthew 7:24-27 is striking. Both ignored wisdom and guidance, building on shaky foundations. This pattern repeats itself, demonstrating the destructive power of sin.

Recognizing sin's subtle yet devastating influence is crucial. We must seek wisdom from God's Word, acknowledging the temptations that surround us.

Beloved, if you get nothing else from this book, please learn this. SIN IS NOT JUST A CHOICE; SIN IS YOUR MORTAL ENEMY!

Sin is a relentless opponent that aims to undermine our relationship with God and others. It can masquerade as tempting choices or desires, but ultimately leads to harm, regret and separation from what's truly important. Sin can distort our thoughts, feelings and actions, causing us to hurt ourselves and those around us.

Beloved, it's essential that we acknowledge sin's presence, separate it from the person it has affected, and confront it as a hostile adversary. By doing so, we can love and support the individual while rejecting harmful actions, preventing sin's corrosive influence from spreading. This discernment empowers us to combat sin's destructive power, fostering healing, redemption, and transformation.

The choice is clear, build on the rock-solid foundation of God's wisdom or risk everything on the shifting sands of human ingenuity. Will we learn from the lessons of Theranos and prioritize God's guidance, or will we succumb to the destructive allure of sin?

Chapter 9
Society & Sin

Let's review and reinforce our understanding of sin and how we think about it. Remember how society and the church often hold differing views about sin.

Again, to many, sin is exclusively seen as a noun – an inherent aspect of human nature, symbolizing flaws and weaknesses inherent in human experience.

Paul Tillich noted, "Sin is not something that happens to us, but something that is with us, as a part of our very being." This perspective frames sin as an intrinsic part of humanity.

Biblically, sin is both a noun and verb, representing a kingdom and an enemy. As a noun, sin is a state of separation from God and a force opposing Him. As a verb, sin encompasses actions and choices rebelling against God's will.

The kingdom of sin seeks to define us by our flaws, weaknesses, and struggles. But God's kingdom offers a radically different narrative – one where our identity is rooted in our creation in God's image. This divine definition transcends our inclinations, traits, and struggles, declaring our inherent worth and dignity.

Society's labels can be suffocating: "ex-con," "crazy," "unwed mother", "addict,", " alcoholic."

These words reduce individuals to their struggles, perpetuating a destructive myth that our worth is tied to our flaws. But what if we're more than our mistakes?

God's kingdom shatters these lies, declaring that our worth exceeds our weaknesses. We're not defined by our flaws but by our inherent value as image-bearers of God. Embracing this truth frees us from sin's distortion, grounding our identities in God's unwavering love.

By recognizing the kingdom of sin's distorted narrative, we can begin to reclaim our true identities and find freedom from the shackles of shame, guilt, and self-doubt. We can learn to see ourselves and others through a different lens, one that reveals our inherent worth, value, and purpose. Only then can we truly embrace our authentic selves and live with dignity, compassion, and hope.

The "I was born this way" mentality can lead to a fixed mindset, where individuals believe they are stuck with their struggles and can't change. This mindset neglects the transformative power of God's love and redemption, which can help us overcome even the most deeply ingrained issues. By recognizing our inherent worth as children of God, we can experience freedom and find a new identity that is not defined by our struggles.

This way of thinking has become so prevalent that even some Christians have adopted it, believing that their natural tendencies and traits define their identity. However, this mindset is in stark contrast to the biblical teaching that our identity is found in Christ and that we are new creations in Him.

Excuses like "I was born this way" or "It's just my personality" hinder personal growth and accountability. Phrases like "I'm naturally jealous" or "I have a quick temper" shift focus from responsibility to fatalism.

Walt Heyer's story exemplifies the complex intersection of faith, identity and personal choice. He underwent gender reassignment surgery in 1983, but after embracing Christianity, Heyer began questioning his decision.

In his book "Trans Life Survivors," Heyer shares his journey of regret and redemption, advocating for caution and spiritual exploration before transition. "The greatest mistake of my life was attempting to change my sex…I deconstructed my male identity and replaced it with a false female identity" (Heyer, "Trans Life Survivors," 2015, p. 13).

Similarly, Laura Perry's story echoes this theme. In 2012, Perry, a former transgender man, detransitioned after experiencing a spiritual awakening. She now speaks out about the importance of exploring faith and identity.

Perry's journey highlights the significance of spiritual exploration in informing life choices. "God's redemption was the catalyst for my detransition…I began to see my identity through His eyes" (Perry, "Transgender to Transformed," 2016, p. 102).

The worldly perspective views sin as inherent flaws, while the Church sees sin as a deliberate choice. However, both perspectives oversimplify sin as a moral issue resolvable through willpower and good deeds.

Scriptures provide clarity: "For the desires of the flesh are against the Spirit, and the desires of the Spirit are against the flesh" (Galatians 5:17, ESV). "Create in me a clean heart, O God, and renew a right spirit within me" (Psalm 51:10, ESV).

To truly comprehend sin, we must recognize its intricate nature. Sin encompasses both inherent tendencies and intentional choices. Dealing with sin requires more than self-effort; it demands divine transformation.

When the Church misunderstands sin, it can lead to a legalistic approach to faith, where salvation and God's favor are seen as rewards for good behavior, rituals, and moral achievements. This perspective emphasizes external actions over internal transformation, prioritizing our efforts to please God over His work in our lives.

A modern example of this is the phenomenon of "Instagram Christianity," where believers present a curated version of their faith online, showcasing their spiritual achievements and good deeds. This can create a culture of competition and comparison, where individuals feel pressure to present a perfect exterior rather than focusing on genuine internal transformation.

Another example is the emphasis on "self-care" and "self-love" as a means of achieving spiritual growth. While self-care is important, when it becomes the primary focus of our faith, it can lead to a self-centered approach to spirituality. We begin to rely on our own efforts to achieve spiritual wellness rather than trusting in God's transformative power.

Take, for instance, the story of Glennon Doyle, a popular author and speaker who built a brand around self-love and self-care. Doyle's message of self-empowerment resonated with many, but ultimately, she admitted that her focus on self-love had become an idol, distracting her from a deeper relationship with God. She realized that her self-sufficiency had become a barrier to genuine spiritual growth and transformation.

In contrast, the Gospel offers a transformative understanding of sin and redemption. It reveals that our salvation and identity are rooted in God's work, not ours. By acknowledging our sins and receiving God's grace, we experience internal transformation, and our actions become a natural response to His love rather than an attempt to earn it.

A works-based religion can be seen in various forms throughout history. For instance, the Pharisaic Judaism of the 1st century believed that strict adherence to the law and rituals could earn them salvation and favor with God. Jesus confronted them for their external focus, emphasizing the need for internal transformation.

Similarly, ancient Roman Catholicism taught that salvation can be earned through faith and good works, indulgences, and sacraments. This led to a system where people could buy their way into heaven or earn forgiveness through external actions. Mormonism also teaches that salvation comes through a combination of faith, good works, and temple rituals, which can lead to a works-based understanding of salvation.

Even some forms of Buddhism emphasize the importance of

good deeds, rituals, and self-effort to achieve enlightenment or nirvana. Buddhism focuses on individual effort; this is a works-based understanding of spiritual progress.

In Islam, salvation is achieved through a combination of faith and good works. Muslims believe that their actions, such as praying five times a day, giving charity, and fasting during Ramadan, will be weighed on the Day of Judgment to determine their eternal destiny.

The Quran teaches that "Whoever does a good deed, it is for his own soul; and whoever does evil, it is against his own soul" *(41:46).*

This emphasis on earning salvation through good deeds is reflected in the Five Pillars of Islam, which are obligations that Muslims must fulfill to demonstrate their devotion.

While faith in Allah and the Prophet Muhammad is essential, it is the performance of these good works that ultimately determines a Muslim's worthiness for paradise. This works-based approach is in contrast to the Christian concept of salvation by faith alone, highlighting a fundamental difference.

You're either living in a works-based religion or a faith-based relationship with God.

Read it again.

You're either living in a works-based religion or a faith-based relationship with God.

This dichotomy is clear: one relies on earning salvation through efforts and good deeds, while the other trusts in God's grace.

THE SIN DECEPTION

In a faith-based relationship, scripture clearly states, "By grace, you have been saved through faith. And this is not your own doing; it is the gift of God, not a result of works, so that no one may boast" (Ephesians 2:8-9 ESV). This emphasizes the role of faith in salvation.

In works-based religion, sin is dealt with through self-effort and good deeds. Individuals strive to overcome sin through personal willpower and moral performance.

We often attempt to overcome sin through various self-efforts, resorting to works-based strategies. These may include setting rigid moral standards, practicing self-discipline, engaging in religious rituals, or performing good deeds to compensate for past wrongs. Some may try to justify or rationalize their actions, shift blame, or rely on self-help methods. Others may turn to introspection, self-reflection or personal growth initiatives. Despite these efforts, scripture reminds us that true transformation comes not from human initiative but divine intervention: "For by grace you have been saved through faith. And this is not your own doing; it Is the gift of God" (Ephesians 2:8-9 ESV).

Faith-based relationships acknowledge sin's complexity, recognizing the human inability to overcome it alone.

A faith-based approach recognizes sin as a pervasive force controlling individuals. It addresses cultural and structural issues enabling sin, emphasizing divine transformation and redemption. This perspective fosters humility, acknowledging human limitations.

In contrast, works-based religion often reduces sin to moral issues solvable through self-effort. This legalistic view can lead to pride and self-righteousness for those appearing to overcome sin, neglecting divine guidance and compassion.

The story of Ted Haggard, a former evangelical pastor, is a poignant example. Haggard was a prominent figure in the evangelical community, known for his strong stance against homosexuality and his advocacy for conservative values.

However, in 2006, he was caught in a scandal involving a male prostitute and methamphetamine.

Haggard's fall from grace was swift and public. He was forced to resign from his church and his leadership roles in the evangelical community. In the aftermath, Haggard spoke publicly about his struggles with sin and his journey towards healing and restoration.

In his book, "The Life-Giving Church," Haggard writes about how his legalistic view of morality contributed to his downfall. He describes how he had become so focused on external behavior modification and moral performance that he had neglected his own need for grace and compassion.

We see the trap of "effort-based" programs in the stories of celebrities like Robert Downey Jr. and Britney Spears, who publicly overcame addiction and personal struggles only to face relapse and public scrutiny. Their experiences highlight the limitations of a legalistic approach to morality, where outward appearances of success can mask ongoing inner struggles. Similarly, the rise and fall of figures like Tony Robbins and Ravi Zacharias, who built their brands on personal development and moral authority, only to face allegations of misconduct, demonstrate the dangers of prioritizing external appearances over genuine transformation and accountability.

The tragic falls of leaders like Tony Robbins and Ravi Zacharias serve as cautionary tales about the devastating consequences of a legalistic approach to morality. When we prioritize external appearances over genuine transformation, we create a culture of hypocrisy and shame. The pressure to maintain a perfect image leads to secrecy and silence, allowing sin to fester and ultimately destroy. The resulting wreckage not only harms individuals but also erodes trust in institutions and disillusioned followers.

Martin Luther, a devout Catholic monk, was consumed by his quest for spiritual perfection. He believed that through intense prayer, fasting, and self-mortification, he could earn God's favor and forgiveness. Luther wrote, "I was a good monk, and I kept the rule of my order so strictly that I may say that if ever a monk could get to heaven by his monkery, it was I."

Luther's days were filled with endless hours of prayer, confession, and penance. He would often say, "I tortured myself with prayers, fasting, and vigils." He believed that his efforts would purify him of sin and bring him closer to God.

However, despite his rigorous efforts, Luther felt like a failure. He was haunted by his own sinfulness and couldn't shake the feeling of guilt. He wrote, "The more I tried to live according to the law, the more I realized I couldn't. I was a sinner, and I couldn't escape my sin."

Luther's legalistic view of morality led him to pride and self-righteousness. He saw himself as a superior monk, judging others who didn't share his level of devotion. He believed that his works would earn him salvation, and he looked down on those who didn't meet his standards.

But then, while studying ***Romans 1:17***, Luther had a breakthrough. He realized that righteousness comes not from our own efforts but from faith in Christ. He wrote, "Here I felt that I was altogether born again and had entered paradise itself through open gates."

Luther's transformation was revolutionary. He began to see his own need for grace and compassion, and his heart was filled with joy and freedom. He wrote, "The gospel is nothing else than the preaching of Christ, in which He is presented as a gift, in which He is offered to us, and in which He is received by us."

Luther's story is a powerful reminder that our works, no matter how good they may seem, cannot earn us salvation. Only through faith in Christ can we find true freedom and forgiveness.

Only by acknowledging sin as both a noun and a verb can we address the root causes of harmful behaviors and promote a culture of healing and restoration. This dual understanding allows us to recognize the inherent flaws that lead to sin while also addressing the actions that separate us from God.

We must understand the kingdom of sin, sin as a noun and sin as a verb.

We have established a solid foundation for understanding sin, its nature, and its impact on humanity. We have seen how sin is not just a singular action but a pervasive state of being that reigns over and holds us captive. We have also explored how sin is a deliberate choice, a conscious decision to rebel against God's commands and design.

Now, as we look forward, we must ask the question: where did this sin come from?

Chapter 10
The Origin Of Sin

The definition of sin has long troubled the human mind. The call to define Sin transcends cultures, religions, and time. From ancient Greek myths to Hindu scriptures, Buddhist teachings to Christian texts, and African folklore to Hollywood narratives, the origin of sin has captivated imaginations. The puzzle that is sin has sparked intense debate among storytellers, theologians, and philosophers, each offering unique explanations for evil, suffering, and moral corruption.

The question that always creates as much controversy is, "What is sin? Where did sin come from?"

Various cultures and belief systems propose distinct accounts. In Christianity, the serpent's whisper in the Garden of Eden marks sin's beginning. Hinduism blames Maya, the illusionary force deceiving humans. Buddhism traces sin to Tanha, craving and attachment. Greek mythology recounts Promethean defiance. These explanations reflect humanity's enduring quest to comprehend sin's presence.

Understanding sin's origins encourages self-reflection, inviting individuals to confront their own flaws and desires. By exploring diverse perspectives, we gain insight into the complexities of human nature. Embracing this knowledge fosters empathy, compassion and personal growth.

Remember when I wrote that the Bible was the ultimate authority on sin?

The Bible provides a clear answer, tracing the origin of sin back to the Garden of Eden and the disobedience of Adam and Eve. This pivotal moment in human history marked the entrance of sin into the world, setting in motion a chain of events that would shape the course of humanity.

As we delve into the story of Adam and Eve, we will explore how sin emerged from a desire for autonomy and self-determination, a desire to be like God. We will see how this desire led to a choice that had far-reaching consequences, consequences that we still grapple with today.

In the next stage of our journey, we will explore the biblical account of the fall, examining the events leading up to it, the consequences that followed, and the ways in which it continues to shape our understanding of sin and humanity. We will also consider the implications of this story for our own lives, exploring how it shapes our understanding of ourselves and our place in the world.

Why did they disobey? What drove them to reject God's goodness and sin?

Augustine of Hippo said, "Sin is not a thing, but a non-thing, a negation, a refusal, a deprivation."

Sin is not a created thing but a corruption of God's good creation.

Understanding the origin of sin also helps us recognize our own propensity for sin and our need for God's mercy. As the apostle Paul wrote, "For all have sinned and fall short of the glory of God" *(Romans 3:23).*

The story of the Fall in Genesis 3 reveals that sin is not just an individual action but a turning away from God in the heart.

By exploring the origin of sin, we can better understand our own struggles with sin.

As C.S. Lewis said, "The Fall is the only way to understand human nature, and the only way to understand the Fall is to understand human nature."

Genesis 3:1-7 (ESV)

Now, the serpent was more crafty than any other beast of the field that the Lord God had made. He said to the woman, "Did God actually say, 'You shall not eat of any tree in the garden'?"

And the woman said to the serpent, "We may eat of the fruit of the trees in the garden, but God said, 'You shall not eat of the fruit of the tree that is in the midst of the garden, neither shall you touch it, lest you die.'"

But the serpent said to the woman, "You will not surely die. For God knows that when you eat of it, your eyes will be opened, and you will be like God, knowing good and evil."

So when the woman saw that the tree was good for food and that it was a delight to the eyes, and that the tree was to be desired to make one wise, she took of its fruit and ate, and she also gave some to her husband who was with her, and he ate.

But why?

The Desire for Autonomy is often suggested as the reason.

According to Tim Keller, in his book The Reason for God,

"Adam and Eve's decision to eat the forbidden fruit was a desire for autonomy, a desire to be like God. They wanted to determine good and evil for themselves rather than trusting in God's sovereignty. This desire for self-rule led them to disobey God's clear command, and it's a temptation that we still face today. We want to be in control, to call the shots, to be our own gods. But in doing so, we forget that God's commands are for our good and that our rebellion leads to suffering and separation from Him.

Maybe it was the Deception of Self-Sufficiency, as noted by John Piper in "Desiring God."

"Adam and Eve's sin was not just about disobeying a rule, but about believing a lie. Satan deceived them into thinking that they needed to be self-sufficient and that they needed to take matters into their own hands. They believed that God was holding out on them, that He was not good. But the truth is that God had already given them everything they needed. They were already created in His image, already living in paradise. Their sin was a failure to trust in God's goodness, a failure to trust that He had their best interests at heart. And that's a failure that we still struggle with today."

In 2019, the American basketball player D.J. Wagner was offered a lucrative contract to play for a Chinese team. However, he was told that he would have to abstain from speaking publicly about his Christian faith. Wagner was faced with a choice: would he prioritize his faith and risk losing the contract and the financial benefits that came with it? Or would he compromise his values and hide his faith in order to advance his career?

What would you do? Millions of dollars to deny your faith publicly… come on, what would you do?

In the end, Wagner chose to stand firm in his faith and declined the contract.

In 2021, a Christian businessman, David Green, the founder of Hobby Lobby, chose to obey God over personal gain. Green had been ordered by the US government to provide health insurance coverage for abortion-inducing drugs to his employees under the Affordable Care Act. However, due to his strong Christian beliefs, Green refused to comply, even though it meant facing significant fines and penalties.

Green chose to obey God's teachings over personal gain, stating, "We're not trying to be a Christian company; we're just trying to be a company that's run by Christians." Hobby Lobby ultimately won a Supreme Court case in 2014, allowing them to opt out of providing the controversial coverage.

David Green chose to put his faith above financial gain, standing firm in his beliefs even in the face of adversity. His decision reflects the biblical principle of obedience to God's teachings, even when it's difficult or costly.

Beloved, think about David Greens heart. How do you think his heart is oriented? David wasn't following a rule or making a political statement, David was keeping his eye on God and trying to live in a way that honors that relationship.

It's not about rules; that is a religion... it's about your heart and your relationship.

As the COVID-19 pandemic swept the nation, thousands of individuals found themselves at a crossroads, forced to choose between their careers and their deeply held faith convictions.

Pause again for a moment, beloved; think about your life and the world you live in.

Do you know someone who had to make a hard choice because of Covid?

Chad Pecknold, a respected professor at Aquinas College, had spent years teaching and mentoring students. However, when the college announced its COVID-19 vaccine mandate, Pecknold knew he had to make a difficult decision. As a devout Catholic, he objected to the use of abortion-derived cell lines in vaccine development and believed that taking the vaccine would violate his faith's teachings on bodily autonomy. Despite his love for teaching, Pecknold chose to leave his job, prioritizing his faith over his academic career.

Again, what would you do? Would you violate your faith for a career?

Across the country, Kim Chill, a dedicated nurse with over 20 years of experience, faced a similar dilemma. When her hospital mandated the COVID-19 vaccine, Chill refused to comply, citing her Christian beliefs. Her decision came at a great personal cost, as she was fired from her position. Yet, Chill remained resolute, convinced that standing by her faith was more important than her career.

THE SIN DECEPTION

Would you risk getting fired over your faith?

Their stories serve as a testament to the power of faith in the face of adversity, highlighting the complex choices individuals must make when their deeply held beliefs conflict with the demands of the world around them.

The choice to trust and obey God is not just a grand gesture reserved for life's major crossroads. It's a daily decision that plays out in the everyday moments we often overlook. When we're stuck in traffic, we're faced with a choice: respond with anger or patience. When we're tasked with a difficult project at work, we can choose to grumble and complain or trust God's sovereignty and provision. Even our conversations are an opportunity to trust and obey God as we decide whether to gossip or speak life and encouragement.

These everyday decisions may seem insignificant, but they reveal the true condition of our hearts. By choosing to trust and obey God in these moments, we build a strong foundation for when the bigger decisions come. We develop a habit of surrender, a reflex of faith, and a heart that is continually surrendered to God's will.

Beloved, our faith requires us to make difficult decisions and prioritize our relationship with God above all else.

According to the Biblical account, Adam and Eve's disobedience marked a pivotal turning point in human history, the event known as "The Fall." This transformative moment saw the first humans transition from a state of innocence and harmony with God to a state of sin and separation. But what was this original state of grace like?

Chapter 11
Before The Fall

In the Garden of Eden, Adam and Eve experienced the ultimate blessing of walking with God. This intimate relationship was characterized by regular fellowship, with God Himself coming to walk with them in the cool of the day. As the Bible says, "The Lord God took the man and put him in the Garden of Eden to work it and keep it" *(Genesis 2:15, ESV).* This was no ordinary stroll but a divine encounter where God shared His presence and His heart with His beloved creation.

As Adam and Eve walked with God, they experienced the joy of unbroken fellowship, untainted by sin or shame. They knew God's goodness and love in a way that was unfiltered by the distortions of sin. In the words of Jonathan Edwards, "The presence of God is the happiness of the soul." In the Garden, Adam and Eve knew this happiness in its purest form.

Scripture paints a picture of a sanctuary where God's presence was palpable, where His voice was heard, and where His love was experienced in its fullness. As Psalm 16:11 says, "You make known to me the path of life; in your presence, there is fullness of joy; at your right hand are pleasures forevermore" (ESV). In the Garden, Adam and Eve knew this path of life, this fullness of joy, and these pleasures that come from walking with God.

In this state of original grace, Adam and Eve experienced the ultimate blessing of communion with God. As Charles Spurgeon said, "Fellowship with God is the very essence of heaven." In the Garden, they knew this essence, this heavenly fellowship.

In this original state, Adam and Eve lived in perfect harmony with God and with each other, unmarred by shame, guilt, or fear. Their relationship with God was marked by trust, obedience, and love, and their relationship with each other was characterized by unity and mutual respect.

In the Garden of Eden, Adam and Eve existed in a state of innocence, untainted by sin or shame. This innocence was characterized by a lack of knowledge of good and evil, as *Genesis 2:17* says, "But of the tree of the knowledge of good and evil you shall not eat, for in the day that you eat of it you shall surely die" (ESV). They didn't know what sin was, and they didn't know what it meant to disobey God.

Imagine that there is ignorance of good and evil. None of their actions were measured against some moral code; they didn't have rules or regulations to follow. They didn't have systems in place to prevent harm or trespass. They didn't worry about saying something wrong or being misunderstood. They didn't fear being yelled at or shamed for making a mistake. They didn't judge themselves against some image of how it "should be." They didn't even think about sin…. Seriously, they didn't even count calories. All they knew was God and His goodness.

Their innocence was also marked by a lack of shame or guilt. As *Genesis 2:25* says, "And the man and his wife were both naked and were not ashamed" (ESV).

Again, beloved, imagine standing in front of another person naked and completely exposed. Nothing is hidden; nothing is covered. And I am not just talking about skin here.

Shame wasn't a part of their world and do you know why? Because sin wasn't a part of their world.

Exposing another Lie that Binds: The Body is an Instrument of Shame

Another pervasive deception perpetuated by the kingdom of sin is that our bodies are instruments of shame. This falsehood assaults our self-worth, distorting God's majestic design. In reality, our bodies are magnificent gifts from God, crafted with precision and purpose.

Each of God's creations, including our bodies, reflects His precise perfection. Psalm 139:14 says, "I praise you, for I am fearfully and wonderfully made. Wonderful are your works; my soul knows it very well." Our unique physical characteristics, skills and talents are intentionally designed to glorify God. Every life matters because every life is created by God, bearing His divine signature (Genesis 1:27, Psalm 139:13-16).

Embracing this truth liberates us from shame and self-condemnation. 1 Corinthians 6:19-20 reminds us, "You are not your own, for you were bought with a price. So glorify God in your body." Our bodies, regardless of appearance or ability, are instruments of worship crafted to honor God. By acknowledging our bodies as gifts, we reclaim our identity as beloved children of God, fearfully and wonderfully made for His glory (Romans 8:14-16, 1 Peter 3:3-4).

Adam and Eve were unselfconscious and unembarrassed, with no sense of wrongdoing or fear of judgment. This innocence was a gift from God, allowing them to enjoy a deep and intimate relationship with Him and with each other.

Adam and Eve were like a mirror, reflecting God's goodness and love without self-awareness or self-consciousness. They were simply living in the moment, enjoying God's presence and provision.

Their Innocence was also characterized by a sense of trust and obedience. They trusted God's word and obeyed His commands without question or hesitation.

As ***Psalm 119:30*** says,

"I have chosen the way of faithfulness; I set your rules before me."
(ESV).

Adam and Eve chose the way of faithfulness, setting God's rules before them and walking in obedience.

In this state of innocence, Adam and Eve were like children, trusting and dependent on their Heavenly Father.

As Jesus said,

"Truly, I say to you, unless you turn and become like children, you will never enter the kingdom of heaven."

– (Matthew 18:3, ESV).

Adam and Eve were like children, enjoying the blessings of the kingdom without the burden of sin or shame.

"The soul is born free, but it is caught and enslaved by the world's deceit."

– Hans Ur von Balthasar (on the loss of innocence)

The Bible tells us, "They walked with God in the Garden, enjoying His presence."

What a perfect description of the intimate relationship Adam and Eve had with God In the Garden of Eden.

Adam and Eve got to enjoy God's presence and companionship. Living in harmony with God's will and purposes allowed them to experience God's guidance and direction. Having open and honest communication with God is part of being in a state of Grace.

"The walking was not merely a physical activity but a metaphor of their spiritual and intimate relationship with God."

(David Guzik)

"The fact that they walked with God indicates a level of trust, fellowship, and friendship that is hard to comprehend."

(John MacArthur)

In the Garden of Eden, Adam and Eve's relationship was a beautiful and untainted reflection of God's design. Their bond was pure, unblemished, and uncontaminated by the corrosive effects of sin. Free from the shackles of guilt, shame, and fear, they enjoyed a relationship that was characterized by mutual respect, trust, and love.

As the Bible says, "Therefore a man shall leave his father and his mother and hold fast to his wife, and they shall become one flesh" *(Genesis 2:24, ESV).* Adam and Eve's relationship was a picture of unity and harmony, a true embodiment of the phrase "one flesh." They were two souls, united in their love for each other and for God, without the divisions and conflicts that would later arise.

Their relationship was also free from the destructive influences of selfishness and pride. They were not consumed by their own needs and desires but rather lived in a state of mutual submission and love. As the apostle Paul would later write, "Submit to one another out of reverence for Christ" *(Ephesians 5:21, ESV).* Adam and Eve's relationship was a beautiful picture of this mutual submission, a testament to the beauty and harmony of God's design.

In this pristine state, Adam and Eve didn't struggle with self-doubt or insecurity, for they were completely secure in their relationship with God. They didn't need to prove themselves or earn their worth, for they knew they were beloved and accepted just as they were. Their identity was rooted in their connection with God, and from that foundation, they lived in perfect freedom and joy.

Adam and Eve's lives were a reflection of God's love and grace, a shining example of what it means to live in perfect harmony with the Creator.

Adam and Eve were in perfect relationship with God and with Each other. They were also in a perfect relationship with creation.

In the Garden of Eden, Adam and Eve's relationship with

creation was a beautiful expression of harmony and stewardship. Unblemished by exploitation or harm, their connection with the natural world was characterized by care, nurturing, and a deep appreciation for its beauty. As God commanded, they exercised dominion over creation, but not in a way that was oppressive or harmful. Rather, their stewardship honored God and reflected a profound understanding of their place within the grand tapestry of creation.

In this idyllic setting, Adam and Eve tended to the earth with reverence and respect, recognizing that God is the creator of all of it all. They had their role as gardeners in the Garden that God planted. Their relationship with creation was marked by stewardship. They acted in harmony with the land, the rivers, and the creatures that inhabited them, reflecting the very character of God who created them.

The harmony between Adam and Eve and the natural world was a beautiful expression of God's design. The Bible declares, "The earth is the Lord's and the fullness thereof, the world and those who dwell therein." They understood that creation belonged to God, and their role was to steward it with care and enjoy its beauty. This harmony was a testament to the goodness of God's creation and a reflection of His character.

Today, we can find inspiration in individuals like Brother Alfred Brousseau, a Benedictine monk who tends to the gardens at the Monastery of the Holy Cross in Chicago. He sees his work as a way to care for God's creation and find joy in the beauty of nature. Through his gentle cultivation of the earth, he demonstrates a deep respect for the land and a sense of wonder at the beauty of God's creation.

Adam and Eve's trust in God's provision and guidance was a hallmark of their pre-fall relationship. They had complete confidence in His sovereignty and goodness, knowing that He would meet all their needs. As *Psalm 23* (KJV) beautifully expresses:

"The Lord is my shepherd; I shall not want. He maketh me to lie down in green pastures: He leadeth me beside the still waters. He restoreth my soul: He leadeth me in the paths of righteousness for his name's sake.

Adam and Eve lived out this truth, relying on God's abundant provision and guidance. Free from worry and anxiety, they rested in the knowledge that their loving Creator cared for them. They didn't strive or struggle to provide for themselves but instead trusted in God's goodness and generosity. Their trust was rooted in a deep understanding of God's character, knowing Him as a loving Father who desired only the best for them.

A beautiful example of this trust is the story of George Müller, a Christian missionary who cared for over 10,000 orphans in the 19th century. Müller trusted God to provide for their needs daily, often seeing miraculous provision. He wrote, "The Lord will provide" and "God is our Father, and He will take care of us."

Adam and Eve followed God's commands, living in sync with His will and aligning their actions with His purposes.

The beauty of obedience! It's a concept that's often misunderstood, isn't it? We think of obedience as a restrictive, joy-sucking duty, something we have to do because we have to, not because we want to. But what if I told you that obedience is actually a key to unlocking joy? That it's not about following rules, but about following the heart of the One who loves us most?

We are exploring Adam and Eve in the Garden when everything is very good. Their obedience wasn't out of obligation; it was a natural response to their love for God. They recognized His wisdom and goodness, and their hearts were inclined to follow Him. They didn't see obedience as a burden; they saw it as a privilege.

As Augustine said, "Love God and do what you will." When we love God, our hearts are inclined to follow Him, and our obedience becomes a joyous expression of our relationship with Him.

But the kingdom of sin has twisted this idea of obedience, hasn't it? It's told us that obedience is restrictive, that it's about following rules and not following our hearts. It told us that true freedom comes from doing what we want, not from following God.

Yet, as we see in the Bible, true freedom comes from obedience. When we follow God, we find joy, peace, and contentment. We find purpose and meaning.

Let me share the story of Eric Liddell, a Scottish athlete who refused to compete on Sundays during the 1924 Olympics. His faith and obedience to God's commands took precedence over his Olympic dreams. Liddell's trust in God's sovereignty and goodness guided his decisions, and he famously said, "God made me fast, and when I run, I feel His pleasure."

Beloved, did you catch that? Eric felt God's pleasure.

What about you? Is there something you do that you can feel God's pleasure in?

When we follow God's commands, living in sync with His will, we experience the joy of obedience and the peace of alignment with His purposes. Our hearts are freed from the burden of self-will, and we find the liberty to live as He intended.

In the Garden of Eden, Adam and Eve enjoyed a perfect relationship with God, each other, and creation. They walked with God in harmony, trusting His provision and guidance. They followed God's commands, living in sync with His will, and their relationships were untainted by sin. They experienced joy, freedom, and peace, living according to God's design.

Even though Adam and Eve knew God's goodness and love in every aspect of their lives, they walked with Him in the cool of the day, enjoying His presence and guidance. But, as we know, this perfect relationship was destroyed. The tempter, Satan, entered the Garden, seeking to destroy the harmony and trust that existed between God and His creation. He deceived Adam and Eve, tempting them to doubt God's goodness and provision and to seek knowledge and power apart from Him.

As they gave in to the temptation, sin entered the world, and with it, a fundamental change in their relationship with God, each other, and creation. Trust was replaced with doubt, harmony with conflict, and innocence with shame. The Fall marked a turning point in human history, a transition from a state of grace to a state of sin, from trust to distrust, and from harmony to discord. Adam and Eve's choice to disobey God's command had far-reaching consequences, affecting not only their own lives but also the lives of generations to come.

Charles Spurgeon wrote,

"The sin of Adam and Eve was not a small sin, but a sin of epic proportions. It was a sin that shook the very foundations of the universe. When they ate the forbidden fruit, the earth groaned, the heavens wept, and the soul of humanity died. The consequences of that sin were catastrophic: disease, death, and destruction entered the world, and the perfect harmony of creation was shattered."

In the beginning, God created a perfect world where humanity lived in harmony with Him. But then, Adam, the first man, made a choice that would change the course of history forever. He disobeyed God's command, and sin entered the world.

Like a ripple effect, Adam's sin spread to all humanity, condemning every person to be born under the dominion of sin. It was as if a dark shadow had fallen over the earth, separating us from God's love and light.

For centuries, humanity has struggled under the weight of sin, unable to escape its grasp. We are like slaves, bound to a master we couldn't shake.

When Adam and Eve disobeyed God's command, their perfect world was shattered. Their relationship with God was broken, and they experienced shame, fear, and separation from Him. Their relationship with each other became marred by guilt, self-condemnation, and low self-esteem. Their relationship with creation was also damaged, leading to conflict, exploitation, and harm.

As C.S. Lewis wrote, "The Fall is a catastrophe which involved the whole universe, and the repair of it will involve the whole universe."

The tragic fall from grace!

Adam, Eve, what have you done? How could you?

Chapter 12
What Did We Lose?

Adam and Eve's disobedience marked a turning point in human history, a point where sin entered the world and changed everything.

Before the fall, Adam and Eve walked in perfect harmony with God without shame or guilt. They were naked, but they didn't know it. They didn't need to hide or cover themselves. But as soon as they ate the forbidden fruit, everything changed.

Shame and guilt crept in, and they realized they were naked. They sewed fig leaves together to cover themselves, trying to hide from God and from each other.

As the Bible says, "Then the eyes of both of them were opened, and they knew they were naked; and they sewed fig leaves together and made themselves coverings" *(Genesis 3:7).*

This moment marked the beginning of the kingdom of sin, a kingdom built on shame, guilt, and fear.

Shame and nakedness, as a result of the fall, have had a horrific impact on humanity, manifesting in a myriad of modern problems. We struggle with self-esteem issues, feeling inadequate, unworthy, and unlovable, constantly striving for validation. Our sense of identity is fragile, as we seek self-worth in external sources like social media likes or material possessions. We're haunted by feelings of inadequacy and self-doubt, leaving us vulnerable to anxiety, depression, and self-sabotage. Our self-worth is fragile, and we often believe we're not enough, that we're failures, and that we don't measure up. This leads to self-criticism and self-condemnation, a constant narrative of negativity. We're afraid to be our true selves, hiding behind masks to avoid rejection, ridicule, or abandonment.

Comparison and competition with others fuel our insecurities, leading to disconnection and isolation. Shame and nakedness distort our understanding of self, driving us to seek validation in all the wrong places.

The Fall also brought about a state of separation from God, who is the source of life and goodness. As God walked in the garden, Adam and Eve hid from His presence, afraid to face Him. This separation meant that they were cut off from God's presence and provision, leading to a state of spiritual death.

The devastating consequences of sin and shame! As commentator Timothy Keller notes, "When we sin, we hide from God, and when we hide from God, we hide from ourselves, and when we hide from ourselves, we hide from our own true selves."

Exposing the Lie: God's Judgment and Wrath

Let's do another exposing the lies that bind. The world and the church would have us believe that God is judgment and wrath. That when we sin, God turns away from us.

The world tells us that if we sin, in whatever way, drinking or sex, or drugs or pornography…. Whatever it is. The world and the church constantly tell us that God is judging us.

When the truth is, Adam and Eve hid from God.

The truth is when we sin, we hide from God. He isn't leaving us. We leave Him.

We turn first with our eyes, then with our hearts, and then with our bodies.

Beloved, God is Abba, our loving Father. Instead of turning away, He pursues us. Genesis 3:9 shows God seeking Adam, calling out, "Where are you?" This demonstrates God's relentless love and desire for connection.

Again, beloved, God is Abba. Father,

He chased after Adam, and He is chasing after you.

Just like Adam and Eve, we often separate ourselves from God when we feel ashamed or guilty. We may not physically hide in the garden, but we hide in other ways.

When overcome with guilt, we often dodge social interactions, seeking refuge in isolation. We devise creative excuses to avoid confronting others, hoping to escape the discomfort of our conscience.

Common evasions include claiming busyness, canceling plans at the last minute or feigning illness. Some might resort to more elaborate justifications, like pretending to have family emergencies or unexpected obligations.

As the ancient proverb goes, "The guilty flee where no man pursueth." This witty saying highlights our tendency to hide when burdened by guilt, even when no one is actively pursuing us.

Guilt-induced hiding can also manifest in more subtle ways, such as avoiding eye contact, changing subjects or withdrawing emotionally. We might become masters of diversion, redirecting conversations to sidestep our own culpability.

Elbert Hubbard humorously captured this sentiment: "To avoid criticism, do nothing, say nothing, and be nothing." While tongue-in-cheek, his words underscore our propensity to hide when feeling guilty. By acknowledging these tendencies, we can begin to confront our guilt head-on and cultivate authenticity in our relationships.

It is no better for the Christian. We avoid prayer or Bible reading, feeling too unworthy to approach God. We miss church services or small group meetings, feeling too guilty to face others or God. We replace intimacy with God with other things, like social media or entertainment, to distract ourselves from our feelings of separation.

As John Piper writes, "Sin and shame drive a wedge between us and God, leading us to hide and avoid His presence." We rationalize our sin, downplaying its significance or convincing ourselves that God is too busy or uninterested to care. Or, we blame others or circumstances, just like Adam did, rather than taking responsibility for our actions.

But here's the good news: God, like the good father He is, comes for His children. He seeks us out, even when we're hiding in the shadows of shame and guilt. He calls us back to Himself, offering forgiveness, restoration, and reconciliation.

As Augustine said, "God is always seeking us, even when we are not seeking Him." He longs to restore our relationship with Himself, to clothe us in righteousness and holiness, and to bring us back into the garden of His presence.

In the Garden of Eden, God confronted Adam and Eve about their disobedience, but instead of taking responsibility, they shifted the blame.

Adam blamed Eve, saying, "The woman whom you gave to be with me, she gave me the fruit, and I ate" *(Genesis 3:12, ESV).* Eve, in turn, blamed the serpent, saying, "The serpent deceived me, and I ate" *(Genesis 3:13, ESV).* However, God held them both accountable for their actions, recognizing that they had chosen to disobey Him.

For centuries, the perception of God has been skewed, leading to a distorted understanding of His true nature. Both Christians and non-Christians often view God as a distant, rule-giving judge, quick to punish and condemn. This misconception portrays God as cruel and vengeful, striking fear into the hearts of many.

However, this image couldn't be further from the truth. The Bible reveals a different God, a loving Father who desires a deep, personal relationship with His children. He is Abba, the Aramaic term Jesus used to address God, meaning "Daddy" or "Papa." This intimate term conveys a sense of warmth, love, and approachability.

God's love is not based on our performance or obedience to rules. Rather, it is an unconditional, unwavering love that accepts us as we are. He loves us first before we even acknowledge Him.

By misunderstanding God's character, we risk missing out on the transformative power of His love. When we see God as Abba, we begin to experience freedom from fear, guilt, and shame. We discover a God who delights in our presence, who desires to guide and empower us, and who longs to shower us with His goodness.

Let us shatter the distorted image of God and embrace the truth. Let us come to know Abba, the loving Father who beckons us to His embrace. As we do, we will find ourselves transformed by His love, living lives marked by joy, peace, and hope.

Adam and Eve have sinned and God will now address them.

God pronounced curses on the serpent and the land; He did not curse Adam and Eve themselves. This distinction is crucial, as it highlights God's desire to restore humanity rather than perpetuate shame and condemnation. The curse is often mistakenly attributed to Adam and Eve, but God's words were directed at the serpent and the land, not at the couple. This subtle yet important distinction underscores God's merciful and redemptive nature, even in the face of disobedience.

After the fall, God's primary desire was to restore humanity, not condemn or harm. This truth is evident in Genesis 3:15, where God promises a redeemer to reconcile humanity with Himself. Despite Adam and Eve's disobedience, God seeks to revive their relationship.

God's nature is often misunderstood as solely judgmental and wrathful. However, Scripture reveals a loving Father who yearns for reconciliation. Psalm 103:13-14 says, "As a father shows compassion to his children, so the Lord shows compassion to those who fear him."

THE SIN DECEPTION

God's discipline is corrective, not destructive.

We still see the effects of sin and shame separating us from each other. When we make mistakes or experience failure, we often shift blame onto others, just like Adam did with Eve.

The tendency to shift blame and point fingers at others is a pervasive issue in today's society. We see it in our personal relationships, social media, and even in the way we approach politics and social justice. But this mindset has its roots in the earliest days of humanity, as demonstrated by Adam and Eve's response to sin.

When confronted by God about their disobedience, Adam blamed Eve, and Eve blamed the serpent (***Genesis 3:12-13***). This victim mentality has been passed down through the ages, and we see it manifesting in our culture today.

Consider the rise of "victim culture," where individuals and groups seek to garner sympathy and leverage by claiming victim status. We see this in the way some people respond to criticism or accountability, immediately playing the victim card to deflect responsibility.

Think about how, when faced with allegations of misconduct, some public figures blame the media, their political opponents, or even the victims themselves.

This blame-shifting mentality prevents us from taking ownership of our actions, learning from our mistakes, and growing as individuals. It also hinders meaningful dialogue, accountability, and progress.

We must recognize the root of this issue – our own sin and desire to avoid responsibility.

We hide behind excuses or justifications rather than taking responsibility. Shame isolates us from others, fearing rejection or judgment. We break relationships or abandon the community rather than seek restoration. We focus on self-preservation rather than seeking forgiveness and healing. Just as in the Garden, God still seeks to restore us rather than condemn us.

This is a good time to review what God actually said.

To Eve, God decreed,

Genesis 3:16

"I will greatly multiply your pain in childbearing; in pain, you shall bring forth children, yet your desire shall be for your husband, and he shall rule over you."

Let's read Henry's commentary.

"This curse affects Eve's relationships, both with God and with Adam. Childbearing, which was previously a joy, will now be accompanied by pain. Additionally, Eve's desire for Adam will be met with his rule over her, indicating a shift in their relationship from equality to patriarchy." (Matthew Henry's Commentary)

This is a great time for exposing the Lies that Bind: Unpacking Patriarchy.

Historically, patriarchy has been wrongly attributed to God's design, perpetuating a distorted view of biblical teachings. This misconception has led to the oppression of women, reinforcing harmful gender roles. However, Scripture reveals that patriarchy emerged as a consequence of sin and the curse, not God's original intent.

Genesis 3:16-17 illustrates the consequences of sin, where God says to Eve,

Your desire shall be for your husband, and he shall rule over you."

This verse describes the effects of the fall, not God's pre-sin plan.

The Hebrew word "teshuvah" (desire) implies a longing to control or dominate, resulting from the broken relationship between men and women.

Beloved, did you catch that…. The Bible says that Eve will desire control and domination.

Pause for a moment and think about your life and the world you live in. In the kingdom of sin, woman dominate and control their husbands.

That is part of what happened in the fall. Eve is now worried about herself at the expense of Adam.

Eve is no longer interested in mutual submission.

It goes both ways. Adam no longer trusts Eve; He doesn't encourage mutual submission. Adam isn't interested in sharing control with Eve. Adam now rules over Eve.

The fall has broken their relationship. Before the fall, Adam and

Eve had their hearts pointed towards God, and that bound them together in His abundance. Beloved, now their hearts are turned towards self.

Similarly, Galatians 3:28 emphasizes equality: "There is neither Jew nor Greek, there is neither slave nor free, there is neither male nor female, for you are all one in Christ Jesus." The Bible promotes mutual submission and respect, not patriarchal domination.

Henry does a good job of illustrating the effects of sin on Eve's relationship with Adam going forward.

While commentary can be incredibly valuable, it's essential to consider the full truth and not rely solely on traditional views.

Many "theologians" suggest that God cursed Adam and Eve, but a closer examination of Scripture reveals that God actually cursed the land and the serpent.

Genesis 3:14

"The Lord God said to the serpent,

'Because you have done this,

Cursed are you, above all, livestock

And above all beasts of the field;

On your belly, you shall go,

And dust you shall eat

All the days of your life.'"

Genesis 3:17

"And to Adam, he said,

'Because you have listened to the voice of your wife

And have eaten of the tree

Of which I commanded you,

"You shall not eat of it,"

Cursed is the ground because of you;

In pain, you shall eat of it all the days of your life.'"

Notice God cursed the ground and the serpent, not Adam and Eve.

This distinction is crucial, as it highlights the depth of God's mercy and grace. Rather than punishing Adam and Eve directly, God chose to curse the land and the serpent, creating a separation between humanity and the natural world.

This nuanced understanding has significant implications for our understanding of sin, shame, and redemption. It suggests that God's plan was not to punish humanity but to restore us to Himself.

The decree on Adam *Genesis 3:17-19*

"Cursed is the ground for your sake; in toil, you shall eat of it all the days of your life. Both thorns and thistles it shall bring forth for you, and you shall eat the herb of the field. In the sweat of your face, you shall eat bread till you return to the ground."

Again, did God curse Adam? No, but let's see what John Calvin had to say.

"Adam's curse affects his work and his relationship with the earth. The ground, which was previously abundant and fruitful, will now bring forth thorns and thistles, requiring Adam to toil and sweat to produce food."

John Calvin's Commentary

He was close, but the Scripture is clear: the curse is on the land. Everything Calvin described should be attributed to the land being cursed, not Adam.

The Curse on the Serpent *Genesis 3:14-15*

"On your belly, you shall go, and you shall eat dust all the days of your life. And I will put enmity between you and the woman, and between your seed and her Seed; He shall bruise your head, and you shall bruise His heel."

"The Serpent's curse affects its physical form and its relationship with humanity. The Serpent will now crawl on its belly, and there will be enmity between it and humanity, culminating in the ultimate victory of Christ over Satan." (Martin Luther's Commentary)

Beloved, just as a side note, I want you to know that crawling on your belly is also a way to describe someone in submission. God never intended for us to submit to the serpent or sin. God said that the serpent would crawl and we are to rule over sin.

The Fall had an immediate impact on Adam and Eve's relationship with each other. They went from being naked and unashamed to being clothed and ashamed *(Genesis 2:25, 3:7, ESV).*

They experienced conflict and blame-shifting, marking a significant change in their relationship with each other.

THE SIN DECEPTION

The Fall was a result of Adam and Eve's choice to disobey God's command and follow Satan's temptation. They sought autonomy and self-determination rather than trusting God's goodness and provision. This downward movement from their original state to a flawed and broken one is a powerful warning that conveys the gravity of sin's consequences and the depth of humanity's need for redemption.

If Adam and Eve were in close communion with God in the Garden of Eden, a paradise planted for them by God Himself, why did they choose to disobey God?

154

Chapter 13
Satan – The Serpent's True Identity

"The devil's most devilish trick is to persuade people that he doesn't exist."

– C.S. Lewis

Belief in Satan is not a matter of opinion; it's a matter of biblical truth. The Bible unequivocally declares Satan's existence, and dismissing this reality can have spiritual consequences. For those who acknowledge Satan's presence, it's crucial to ensure our understanding aligns with Scripture.

Not believing in Satan can lead to spiritual complacency, vulnerability to deception and ignoring spiritual warfare. This mindset overlooks the destructive power of Satan's influence.

Some argue Satan is a myth or symbol, representing human evil or a relic of outdated theology. However, this perspective disregards historical accounts of spiritual warfare, personal experiences of believers and the Bible's clear teachings.

The biblical account of the Fall reveals the serpent as Satan, God and humanity's adversary. Revelation 12:9 unmasked him: "The great dragon, ancient serpent, devil and Satan, deceiver of the whole world"

(ESV). Paul warns in 2 Corinthians 11:3: "The serpent deceived Eve, and your thoughts may be led astray from devotion to Christ" (ESV).

Beloved, pay attention to Satan's deceptive nature, highlighting his role in leading humanity astray.

Satan's Origin and Fall

Satan, once a perfect angel, rebelled against God.

Isaiah 14:12-15 describes his fall: "You fell from heaven, Day Star, son of Dawn! Cast down to earth, you laid low nations." His prideful ambition led to expulsion. Ezekiel 28:12-17 details Satan's perfection, beauty and subsequent fall: "Blameless until unrighteousness corrupted you…Filled with violence, you sinned." Revelation 12:9 reaffirms: "The ancient serpent, devil and Satan, thrown down to earth with his angels."

The Fall of Satan

Satan, once a majestic and perfect angel, harbored a devastating secret: pride. His heart swelled with ambition, fueled by an insatiable desire for power and self-elevation. Isaiah 14:13-14 exposes his treacherous plan: "You said in your heart, 'I will ascend to heaven; above the stars of God, I will set my throne on high.'" Satan's rebellious cry echoed through the heavens, shaking the very foundations.

His stunning beauty and perfection blinded him to God's sovereignty. Satan coveted God's throne, seeking equality with his Creator.

THE SIN DECEPTION

Ezekiel 28:12-17

"Son of man, raise a lamentation over the king of Tyre, and say to him, Thus says the Lord God:

"You were the signet of perfection,

Full of wisdom and perfect in beauty.

You were in Eden, the garden of God;

Every precious stone was your covering,

Carnelian, topaz, and jasper,

Diamond, beryl, and onyx,

Sapphire, emerald, and jasper,

Lapis lazuli, turquoise, and amethyst;

The workmanship of your settings and sockets

Was in you;

On the day you were created, they were prepared.

You were an anointed guardian cherub;

I placed you; you were on the holy mountain of God;

In the midst of the stones of fire, you walked.

You were blameless in your ways.

From the day you were created,

Till unrighteousness was found in you.

In the abundance of your trade

You were filled with violence in your midst,

And you sinned;

So, I cast you as a profane thing

From the mountain of God,

And the guardian cherub drove you out

From the midst of the stones of fire."

Reveals the depth of his pride, documenting his tragic fall from perfection.

Humanity unwittingly played a role in Satan's rebellion. Genesis 3:1-7 recounts the deception: Satan tempted Eve, introducing sin into the world. Humanity's fall sealed our fate, binding us to Satan's rebellion. The earth suffered alongside humanity, subjected to the curse of sin.

Satan's insurgency sparked catastrophic consequences. Expulsion from heaven marked the beginning of his eternal separation from God. Corruption consumed humanity, and the earth bore the scars of rebellion. Revelation 12:7-9 chronicles Satan's downfall: "And the great dragon was thrown down, that ancient serpent, who is called the devil and Satan, the deceiver of the whole world."

Exposing another Lie that Binds – Satan's Deceptive Snare

Satan's most cunning deception is that he desires your allegiance, promising fleeting fame, fortune and power in exchange for your eternal soul.

With an eternal and unquenchable fury, Satan hates you more than any other creation of God! His ultimate goal is not to elevate you but to annihilate the very Image of God within you, leaving you shattered and soulless.

Satan's insatiable thirst for destruction knows no bounds! He seeks to unleash unimaginable torment, shatter your spirit and extinguish your faith. His dark ambition is to claim your soul.

Satan's primary objective is to viciously erase the divine imprint within you, grotesquely distorting God's reflection and rendering you useless for eternal purposes.

Do not be deceived; Satan's promises are hollow and poisonous! Serving him ensures eternal damnation, agonizing separation from God and the loss of your true identity.

We now live in a world under the curse of sin, where darkness reigns and evil dominates. Humanity is held captive, subjected to Satan's tyranny. Sin has claimed dominion, and death looms over every soul. The earth groans under the weight of corruption.

Beloved, recognizing Satan's tactics and relying on scripture, we can resist his influence and walk in faith, trusting God's sovereignty.

Satan's ultimate objective is to undermine God's sovereignty and sabotage humanity's relationship with Him. Through masterful deception, temptation, and manipulation, Satan seeks to divert humanity from God's design. The temptation of Eve in the Garden of Eden exemplifies this sinister strategy.

In this pivotal encounter, Satan exploited Eve's desires, sowing seeds of doubt and rebellion. By distorting God's command and promising forbidden knowledge, Satan cunningly led Eve to disobey, introducing sin into the world.

Look. Closey at what Satan promises and what Eve desires. Remember, first, we sin with the eyes, then with the heart and then with the body.

 See if you can pick out the moment her eyes left God.

Genesis 3:1-6

"Now the serpent was more cunning than any beast of the field that the Lord God had made. He said to the woman, 'Did God actually say, "You shall not eat of any tree in the garden"?'

The woman said to the serpent, 'We may eat of the fruit of the trees in the garden, but God said, "You shall not eat of the fruit of the tree that is in the midst of the garden, neither shall you touch it, lest you die."'

But the serpent said to the woman, 'You will not surely die. For God knows that when you eat of it, your eyes will be opened, and you will be like God, knowing good and evil.'

So when the woman saw that the tree was good for food and that it was a delight to the eyes, and that the tree was to be desired to make one wise, she took of its fruit and ate, and she also gave some to her husband who was with her, and he ate.

Then, the eyes of both were opened, and they knew that they were naked. And they sewed fig leaves together and made themselves loincloth."

This deception sparked a spiritual battle between God and Satan, with humanity trapped in the crossfire.

Satan's malice toward humanity and God is evident in his actions. He doesn't merely oppose God; he hates humanity, seeking to destroy our relationship with God and creation. His primary goal is to sever our connection with God, corrupting our understanding of His goodness and love.

The serpent's deception serves as a warning to believers to remain vigilant against Satan's insidious schemes. Throughout Scripture, the serpent symbolizes opposition to God's plan. Jesus faced temptation, and Peter urged believers to be alert and resist Satan, who prowls like a roaring lion (1 Peter 5:8).

The consequences of the Fall were catastrophic: spiritual separation from God, physical death, and a distorted relationship with creation. This devastating outcome underscores the urgency of recognizing Satan's tactics and resisting his influence.

Before the fall, nothing died. The world was perfect, and humanity lived in harmony with God and nature. But when sin entered through Adam and Eve's disobedience, death also entered the world.

This was not just physical death but also spiritual death – separation from God.

When Adam and Eve sinned, they felt shame and guilt, and they tried to cover themselves with fig leaves. But God, in His mercy, provided a different covering. He killed an animal, likely a lamb or a goat, and used its skin to clothe Adam and Eve. This was the first death, and it was a sacrifice to pay for their sin.

Death, disease, sickness, aging, and dying – these are all harsh realities that we face in life. But the Bible reveals that they are not natural parts of God's original design. Instead, they are consequences of sin's entrance into the world. When Adam and Eve disobeyed God, they unleashed a cascade of suffering and death that affected us all. Our bodies, once perfect and strong, now succumb to weakness, illness, and, ultimately, death. The Bible says that "sin entered the world through one man, and death through sin" *(Romans 5:12).*

As a result of sin, our bodies are subject to decay and deterioration. We age, we get sick, and we die. But it's not just physical death that's the problem – sin also brings spiritual death, separating us from God and His eternal life.

By killing the animal and covering Adam and Eve's shame, God showed that sin requires payment and that He is willing to provide that payment Himself.

The serpent's temptation was rooted in doubt and deception, questioning God's word and His goodness.

The serpent's strategy was to create doubt in Eve's mind about God's word and His character. He asked, "Did God actually say…?"

(Genesis 3:1), implying that God was holding something back or that His command was unreasonable. This doubt led Eve to question God's goodness and provision.

So far, we have covered what sin is, both as a noun and as a verb. We have discussed the kingdom of sin, the system used to promote the kingdom of sin, and some of the deceptions that are meant to expand the dominion of the kingdom of sin and put more people under its bondage. We have covered the origin of sin, the act of disobedience, the state of innocence, and the fall. We have covered the serpent's part in the fall and what it cost us.

As we explore the narrative of the Garden of Eden, a profound question arises: Have I sinned and fallen away from God?

The answer lies in understanding the far-reaching consequences of Adam and Eve's disobedience. Through their sin, death entered the world, and its impact resonates throughout humanity.

The apostle Paul Illuminates this truth in *Romans 5:12 (ESV)*: "As sin came into the world through one man and death through sin, and so death spread to all men because all sinned." This verse reveals the sobering reality that sin's entrance into the world affected us all.

The Bible teaches that through Adam's sin, humanity inherited a sinful nature, prone to rebellion against God. This inherent inclination towards sin separates us from our Creator, leading to spiritual death and physical mortality.

The Bible unequivocally states that sin is a universal problem that affects every person who has ever lived. The apostle Paul writes, "For all have sinned and fall short of the glory of God" *(Romans 3:23,*

ESV). This verse leaves no room for exceptions or excuses; sin is a fundamental aspect of the fallen human condition.

In *Psalm 53:3,* David laments, "There is no one who does good, not even one" (ESV). This somber assessment highlights the depth of humanity's sinful nature. We often try to justify or downplay our sins, but the Bible refuses to sugarcoat the truth.

We see evidence of sin all around us. People lie to avoid conflict or gain an advantage, envy others' success or possessions, dishonor parents or authority figures, covet material possessions or wealth, and satisfy sinful desires at the expense of others. These everyday thoughts, words, and actions contradict God's character and demonstrate the pervasive nature of sin.

As the prophet Isaiah confessed, "We have all become like one who is unclean, and all our righteous deeds are like a polluted garment" *(Isaiah 64:6, ESV).*

We must examine our hearts. It's crucial to acknowledge the universal truth that all have sinned. The Bible warns, "There is no one who does not sin" *(1 Kings 8:46, NIV),* and "all have turned aside, together they have become worthless" *(Romans 3:12, ESV).* Our attempts to achieve perfection are futile, as "the heart is deceitful above all things and desperately sick" *(Jeremiah 17:9, ESV).*

We may try to hide behind a façade of righteousness, but our thoughts, words, and actions reveal the truth. We've all fallen short of God's standards, and "there is no one who seeks God" *(Romans 3:11, ESV).* Even our best efforts are tainted by self-interest and pride, leaving us "dead in our trespasses and sins" *(Ephesians 2:1,*

ESV).

The psalmist David confessed, "I know my transgressions and my sin is ever before me" *(Psalm 51:3, ESV).* This honest self-reflection is essential for us to recognize our sins. Let us acknowledge the truth: we have all sinned.

In the words of the apostle John, "If we claim to be without sin, we deceive ourselves, and the truth is not in us. If we confess our sins, he is faithful and just and will forgive us our sins and purify us from all unrighteousness" *(1 John 1:8-9, NIV).*

If we acknowledge that we are sinners with a blood debt over our heads, we need to learn what sin costs us.

The Bible warns, "For the wages of sin is death, but the free gift of God is eternal life in Christ Jesus our Lord" *(Romans 6:23, ESV).*

This death refers not only to physical mortality but also to spiritual separation from our Creator.

Living as a sinner in a fallen world brings a weighty cost. Shame and guilt grip our hearts. Remember in Genesis, where Adam and Eve sewed fig leaves together to cover their nakedness, attempting to hide from God? Our sin separates us from God, as *Isaiah 59:2* declares, "But your iniquities have made a separation between you and your God, and your sins have hidden his face from you so that he does not hear." Damaged relationships, inner turmoil, suffering, and pain are all consequences of sin.

Living as a sinner in a fallen world is a life marked by fear and anxiety as the righteous flee from the wicked. Conflict and strife reign, as ***James 4:1-3,*** says, "What causes quarrels and what causes fights among you? Is it not this that your passions are at war within you? You desire and do not have, so you murder. You covet and cannot obtain, so you fight and quarrel."

Emptiness and discontentment plague us, as Ecclesiastes reveals. Darkness and confusion shroud our minds, and as John 3 states, "And this is the judgment: the light has come into the world, and people loved the darkness rather than the light because their works were evil. For everyone who does wicked things hates the light and does not come to the light, lest his works should be exposed."

As we journey through life, it's easy to get caught up in the hustle and bustle of daily routines and distractions. But in doing so, we often overlook the deepest, most profound aspects of our own hearts. Hidden sin, unchecked and unconfessed, can quietly wreak havoc on our lives, relationships, and spiritual growth.

Reflecting on our lives and uncovering hidden sins is a courageous and necessary act. It requires humility, honesty, and a willingness to confront the darkest corners of our own souls. But the reward is immeasurable. When we open ourselves up completely to the light of God's truth, we invite transformation, healing, and freedom.

The stark reality of our condition is devastating. We are all guilty of sin, living in a fallen world where the kingdom of sin has dominion. Our nature is bent towards wickedness, and we have chosen to sin against God.

As the Bible says, "For all have sinned and fall short of the glory of God" *(Romans 3:23).* Our sin is not just a mistake or an error but a deliberate choice to rebel against God's authority.

We have exchanged the truth of God for a lie, worshipping created things rather than the Creator Himself *(Romans 1:25).* Our hearts are inclined towards evil, and we are prone to wander away from God's path.

But here's the sobering truth: as sinners, we are all bound for death and judgment and hell. We have a problem, a massive, show-stopping disaster of a problem. Sin has separated us from God, and we are unable to bridge the gap on our own.

We are like a ship wrecked on the rocks of sin, unable to go anywhere but down. We are like a patient diagnosed with a terminal illness with no cure in sight. We are like a prisoner trapped in a cell of sin with no key to unlock the door.

If we can't save ourselves and no amount of work can earn salvation, What shall we do?

Chapter 14
Progressive Revelation of God's plan for sin.

Throughout human history, God has progressively revealed His plan to address the problem of sin, demonstrating His patience, love, and desire for redemption.

In the beginning, God dealt with Adam and Eve's sin through personal confrontation and merciful provision. As sin spread, He confronted Cain's violence with a warning and a mark of protection. When sin engulfed the world, God sent the Flood, saving Noah and his family and establishing a new covenant with humanity.

With Abraham, God initiated a covenant of promise, calling a people to Himself and foreshadowing the redemption to come. The Law of Moses brought clarity to God's standards and revealed the need for atonement, which was temporarily satisfied through the sacrifices at the Wilderness Tabernacle and later at the temple in Jerusalem.

With the law, we learned the seriousness of sin and the need for obedience. Yet, despite the law's presence, sin continued to plague humanity. Why did the law prove insufficient in eradicating sin?

The prophets then emerged, calling people to repentance and

faithfulness. But even their powerful messages couldn't completely eradicate sin. What more did God need to do to address this persistent problem?

The exile resulted from Israel's continued disobedience and sin, but even this severe consequence didn't fully resolve the issue. Are you starting to see that sin is a deeply ingrained problem that requires a radical solution?

It's only when we grasp the depth of the problem that we can appreciate the magnitude of God's solution.

As this is a Biblical-focused study on sin, a general recap is in order.

I am providing specific dates in this first then I will explain each period.

In Adam's time (circa 4000 BC), sin entered the world through disobedience, and humanity's relationship with God was severed. The early descendants of Adam offered sacrifices to atone for their sins, but these actions were insufficient to fully restore their relationship with God. As the human population grew, so did sin, leading to a global corruption that prompted God to send the Great Flood in Noah's time (circa 2900 BC). After the Flood, God established a new covenant with Noah, promising never again to destroy the earth with a flood.

In Abraham's time (circa 2000 BC), God introduced the concept of circumcision as a physical sign of His covenant with His people. This marked the beginning of a more formal system of atonement, where sins were forgiven through animal sacrifices and offerings.

During Moses' time (circa 1500 BC), the Law was given, providing a clear framework for understanding sin and its consequences.

The sacrificial system was formalized, and the priesthood was established to mediate between God and His people. In David's time (circa 1000 BC), the kingdom of Israel was established, and the sacrificial system continued to evolve. However, despite these developments, sin persisted, and the kingdom eventually divided.

During the time of the prophets (circa 800-500 BC), God's people were repeatedly called to repentance, but their sin ultimately led to the Babylonian exile (586 BC). In the Second Temple period (515 BC-70 AD), the sacrificial system was reinstated, but the focus shifted from mere ritual observance to a deeper understanding of sin and its consequences.

The prophets emphasized the need for inward transformation and genuine repentance, highlighting the limitations of external rituals in fully addressing the problem of sin.

From the moment sin entered the world through Adam's disobedience, God had a plan to deal with it. And God has a plan to deal with your sin, too. Throughout history, God revealed His plan incrementally, ultimately leading to the perfect solution.

Initially, God addressed sin through direct judgment and mercy, as seen in the stories of Cain and Abel. However, as humanity grew, so did sin, prompting God to send the Great Flood to reset creation.

After the Flood, God established a covenant with Abraham, introducing the concept of atonement through animal sacrifices.

In the Old Testament, God established a system of sacrifices to help His people deal with sin. When someone sinned, they would offer an animal sacrifice to atone for their wrongdoing. For example, if someone lied, they would offer a sinful offering, such as a lamb or a goat, to make amends with God (Leviticus 6:1-7). The idea was that the animal would take the punishment for the person's sin, allowing them to be forgiven and restored to a right relationship with God.

The type of sacrifice varied depending on the sin committed. For instance, if someone committed a serious sin like murder, they would offer a more significant sacrifice, like a bull *(Leviticus 4:1-12)*.

But for lesser sins, like unintentional mistakes, a smaller offering like a dove or a grain offering might be sufficient *(Leviticus 5:5-13).* The sacrificial system was designed to teach God's people about the seriousness of sin and the need for forgiveness, as well as to point forward to the ultimate sacrifice that would one day be made to atone for sin once and for all.

Through the sacrificial system, God's people learned that sin has consequences. They were no happier about killing an animal than you, or I would be, barring cultural differences. The cost was real to them. Sin is so damaging that the Israelites were willing to offer the animal in their place.

In offering sacrifices, they acknowledged their wrongdoing, expressed remorse, and sought restoration with God. This system was a crucial part of God's plan to prepare His people for the coming of the Messiah, who would ultimately fulfill the sacrificial system and provide a perfect solution for sin.

THE SIN DECEPTION

The concept of animal sacrifice in the ancient world can be challenging for modern sensibilities to grasp. Critics often argue that a loving God would never require such brutal practices. However, this perspective fundamentally misunderstands the true purpose of sacrifice. God doesn't delight in sacrifice; He desires obedience. The Hebrew scriptures emphasize this repeatedly, underscoring that sacrifice serves as a vivid reminder of sin's devastating consequences: it costs life.

In the Old Testament, animal sacrifice illustrated the gravity of humanity's rebellion against God. The Israelites' sins necessitated the shedding of innocent blood, foreshadowing the ultimate sacrifice – Jesus Christ. This system wasn't about God's desire for bloodshed but about atonement, substitution, education, and anticipation. Sacrifices temporarily covered sin, allowing humans to approach a holy God, while innocent animals died in place of guilty humans, demonstrating sin's deadly consequences.

This system, formalized in the Law given to Moses, allowed people to temporarily cover their sins. Yet, this cycle of sin, sacrifice, and repetition couldn't fully address the problem.

Through the prophets, God emphasized the need for inward transformation and genuine repentance. The sacrificial system, though inadequate, pointed to the need for a more perfect solution.

Beloved, why couldn't the sacrifice solve the problem? Think about the kingdom of sin. You repent and give up getting drunk; you go to the temple and sacrifice a lamb. They kill the lamb in your place. Your sin is forgiven. On the way home, you run into your friend, who informs you that the drinks are half off at the pub. You say to yourself, they are probably half watered down, too, but what the heck?

If sin is to be dealt with, it must be dealt with in all its forms, fashions, strongholds and dominions. Sin must be defeated once and for all, or it won't be defeated at all.

In the Second Temple period, God's people awaited a Messiah who would finally resolve the sin problem. The Old Testament prophesied this deliverer would bring redemption, forgiveness, and a new covenant.

As God's plan unfolded, we consistently revealed God's desire to reconcile humanity to Himself. The story of sin and redemption is one of God's relentless pursuit of His people, ultimately leading to the perfect solution: the cross.

Beloved, I am trying to show you God's consistent effort to address sin, demonstrating His unwavering commitment to saving humanity.

In the aftermath of humanity's fall, God established a system of sacrifices to foreshadow the coming Messiah. Through animal offerings, God's people acknowledged their sins and expressed remorse. The sacrificial system pointed to the need for a perfect sacrifice to atone for sin.

Centuries later, *Psalm 51:16-17* highlighted the inadequacy of animal sacrifices, saying, "For you will not delight in sacrifice, or I would give it; you will not be pleased with a burnt offering. The sacrifices of God are a broken spirit; a broken and contrite heart, O God, you will not despise." This psalm hinted at the need for a deeper solution, one that would address the heart of humanity's rebellion.

The sacrificial system, though imperfect, served as a temporary solution, allowing God's people to approach Him despite their sins. Leviticus 1:3-4 describes the burnt offering, where a worshiper would offer a male without blemish to atone for their sin. This sacrifice symbolized the need for perfection in approaching God. As the ages passed, God's people offered sacrifices, awaiting the fulfillment of the Messiah's coming.

The sacrificial system illuminated the darkness of humanity's rebellion. Millions of animals were sacrificed to cover sin, yet it was never enough. It could never be enough.

The only hope is in a Messiah who would vanquish sin and its offspring, restoring God's original intent for humanity. In the midst of sin's kingdom, we find solace in the promise of a Messiah to come, who would perfect the sacrificial system and shatter sin's dominion.

These prophecies and others like them fueled the longing hearts of God's people, who waited for the arrival of the One who would bring salvation.

For millennia, the relentless cycle of sin and sacrifice had ensnared humanity, a never-ending loop of guilt and atonement. The shed blood of animals, a temporary salve for the conscience, served as a poignant reminder of the depth of human rebellion. With each passing generation, the futility of this cycle grew more apparent as sin's grip on humanity only tightened.

The Bible describes the condition of man as being lost in sin, separated from God, and trapped in a fallen world. The only hope for humanity is God Himself.

Sin is a destructive force that has ravaged humanity since the fall of Adam and Eve. It's a poison that seeps into every aspect of our lives, causing us to hurt ourselves, others, and our relationship with God. Sin's consequences are devastating: it brings shame, guilt, and fear and ultimately leads to death and separation from God. The Bible says that "all have sinned and fall short of the glory of God" (***Romans 3:23***), meaning that every person has been infected by sin's corruption. Our sinfulness is so deep-seated that we can't escape its grasp on our own.

That's why a final, perfect sacrifice is needed to pay for our sins. But how could any sacrifice, even a perfect one, be enough to cover the sins of the entire world? How could a bull, no matter how flawless, pay for the cumulative guilt of humanity's rebellion? The value of any earthly sacrifice is finite, while the weight of global sin is infinite.

The Old Testament sacrifices were just a shadow of the ultimate sacrifice, pointing to the need for something far greater. Only a sacrifice of infinite worth could satisfy God's justice and fully pay for our sins. This perfect sacrifice would need to be sinless, yet take the blame for our sins; innocent, yet bear the guilt of our rebellion. Only then could God's justice be satisfied and our sin debt be fully paid.

The sacrificial system, with its animal offerings and rituals, was a temporary solution to the problem of sin. But it pointed to a deeper need for a perfect sacrifice, one that would finally and completely forgive sin.

Chapter 15
The Messiah's Promised Arrival

For centuries, the Israelites eagerly anticipated the Messiah's arrival, expecting Him to end the cycle of sin and sacrifice. They longed for a leader who would establish God's kingdom, addressing everyday needs and deepest spiritual longings. This expectation was rooted in ancient prophecies, foretelling a priest-king Messiah who would lead God's people, forgive sins and bring them closer to God.

The Old Testament painted a vivid picture of this coming Messiah. He would be a descendant of Abraham, Jesse and David, born in Bethlehem. He would rule with wisdom and justice, yet surprisingly, also be a suffering servant, bearing the sins of others. King David spoke of a future suffering servant whose hands and feet would be pierced. Isaiah described a coming Messiah who would be despised and rejected yet bear the griefs and sorrows of God's people.

Micah prophesied the Messiah's birth in Bethlehem, while Isaiah foretold His ministry in Galilee. Over 300 Old Testament predictions, or messianic prophecies, confirmed the Messiah's coming. The Israelites expected Him to bring light to nations, free captives, heal the brokenhearted and bring good news to the poor. They sought a new covenant with God, offering redemption and forgiveness.

However, they misunderstood that this would come through sacrifice, not conquest. The sacrificial system temporarily covered sin, but the Israelites felt separated from God and yearned for a solution. Unbeknownst to them, the solution was coming – a humble, sacrificial lamb, not a conquering hero.

In the fullness of time, Jesus arrived, fulfilling these prophecies. His birth in Bethlehem, ministry in Galilee and sacrificial death on the cross answered the Israelites' deepest longings. Jesus brought light to nations, freed captives, healed the brokenhearted and brought good news to the poor. He established a new covenant, offering redemption and forgiveness.

God tested Abraham's faith by asking him to sacrifice his son Isaac, whom he loved dearly, as a burnt offering. Abraham, without hesitation, obeyed God's command, demonstrating his unwavering trust in God's goodness and provision.

Abraham prepared for the journey, taking Isaac and two servants with him. As they approached the designated location, Abraham instructed the servants to wait while he and Isaac proceeded to worship. Isaac, unaware of the true purpose of their journey, asked his father about the lamb for the burnt offering. Abraham's response, "God will provide for himself the lamb" *(Genesis 22:8),* revealed his faith in God's provision.

Upon arriving at the designated location, Abraham built an altar, arranged the wood, and bound Isaac. As he raised his knife to slay his son, an angel of the Lord intervened, instructing Abraham to stop. A ram caught In a nearby thicket was then offered as a substitute sacrifice, symbolizing God's provision.

Beloved, what was the inclination of Abraham's heart? Can you see that as long as you have your eyes on God, Abba always provides?

Abraham and Isaac's story had already laid the groundwork for understanding the significance of sacrifice and redemption. Abraham's willingness to sacrifice his son Isaac and God's provision of a ram as a substitute foreshadowed the ultimate sacrifice that would come later. This narrative established the principle of a substitute sacrifice, where life is given in exchange for life.

Much later, when the Israelites were enslaved in Egypt, God was about to deliver them through a series of plagues. The final plague, the death of every firstborn son, would be a devastating blow to both the Egyptians and the Israelites. However, God instructed Moses to have the Israelites mark their doorposts with the blood of a lamb, which would serve as a sign distinguishing their homes from those of the Egyptians.

On the night of the Passover, each Israelite family was to sacrifice a lamb, applying its blood to the doorposts and lintel of their home. When the angel of death saw the blood, he would "pass over" that house, sparing the firstborn son from death.

The blood on the doorposts served as a substitute for the firstborn son, taking his place as the one to die. This act of obedience and faith in God's command would ultimately lead to the Israelites' salvation from physical death.

In this account, the blood of the lamb represented life given in exchange for life, echoing the earlier story of Abraham and Isaac. The

Passover narrative reinforced the concept of substitutionary sacrifice, where the blood of the lamb provided a substitute for humanity's sin. This theme would continue to unfold, ultimately pointing to the sacrifice of the Lamb of God, who would take away the sin of the world.

John the Baptist's declaration, "Behold, the Lamb of God, who takes away the sin of the world!" *(John 1:29)*, marks the transition to the ultimate sacrifice. Jesus, the Lamb of God, would bring redemption and forgiveness, not just for the Israelites but for the entire world.

As Augustine said, "God has provided a Lamb, a Lamb that is blameless, a Lamb that is spotless, a Lamb that is worthy of God." This Lamb would bridge the gap between humanity and God, a provision that would change the course of history forever.

Chapter 16
The Cross

The cross, a symbol of shame and execution, became the instrument of salvation. Jesus, the Lamb of God, bore the sins of the world, taking upon Himself the punishment we deserved. As Isaiah prophesied, "He was pierced for our transgressions, he was crushed for our iniquities; the punishment that brought us peace was on him, and by whose wounds we are healed" *(Isaiah 53:5).*

This sacrifice was not just a historical event but a cosmic transaction. As John Stott said, "The cross is the proof of God's justice, the demonstration of His love, and the grounds of our salvation."

Through the cross, God reconciled the world to Himself, providing forgiveness and redemption.

As Paul wrote, "God was in Christ reconciling the world to Himself, not counting their trespasses against them" *(2 Corinthians 5:19).*

The sacrificial lamb, once a symbol of temporary atonement, found its ultimate fulfillment in Jesus. As the book of Hebrews so eloquently states:

"For since the law has but a shadow of the good things to come instead of the true form of these realities, it can never, by the same sacrifices that are continually offered every year, make perfect those who draw near. Otherwise, would they not have ceased to be offered since the worshipers, having once been cleansed, would no longer have any consciousness of sins? But in these sacrifices, there is a reminder of sins every year, for it is impossible for the blood of bulls and goats to take away sins.

Therefore, when he comes into the world, he says, 'Sacrifices and offerings you have not desired, but a body have you prepared for me; in burnt offerings and sin offerings you have taken no pleasure.' Then I said, 'Behold, I have come to do your will, O God, as it is written of me in the scroll of the book.'" *(Hebrews 10:1-7, ESV)*

Jesus' sacrifice was the reality that the old covenant sacrifices merely foreshadowed. He declared, "Lo, I have come to do your will, O God," and in doing so, He fulfilled the law and provided a once-for-all atonement for our sins. As the author of Hebrews concludes:

"And every priest stands daily at his service, offering repeatedly the same sacrifices, which can never take away sins. But when Christ had offered for all time a single sacrifice for sins, he sat down at the right hand of God..." *(Hebrews 10:11-12, ESV)*

In Jesus, the symbolic sacrifices of the old found their ultimate fulfillment, providing a permanent solution for humanity's sin problem.

In this, we find hope. As Charles Spurgeon said, "The cross is the foundation of our hope, the fountain of our joy, and the theme of our praise."

No longer would animals be required to atone for sin; instead, the perfect Lamb of God would offer Himself once and for all. This new covenant was established through death as the required sacrifice for sin and resurrection to a restored relationship with God. The final sacrifice would bring forgiveness, redemption, and eternal life to all who put their faith in Him.

184

Chapter 17
Who is this Messiah?

John the Baptist declared, "Behold, the Lamb of God!" pointing to Jesus Christ. The Israelites were waiting for the Messiah, the Anointed One, who would redeem and restore God's people. Jesus is that promised Messiah.

The prophecies were clear, yet the people's vision was obscured by their desires. They yearned for a triumphant warrior, a powerful king, to vanquish Roman rule. But God's purpose transcended earthly conquests. He came to conquer the root of humanity's suffering: sin. God's plan was to liberate humanity from its greatest foe, not just Roman oppression. The true battle was not against flesh and blood but against the darkness that had ensnared humanity.

In the small town of Bethlehem, a child was born, a descendant of Abraham, Jesse, and David. This child, Jesus, was the fulfillment of ancient prophecies, the long-awaited Messiah.

As Jesus grew and ministered, He demonstrated His divine nature. He was a priest like Melchizedek, a prophet like Moses, and a suffering servant who bore the sins of others. His teachings were unlike anything the people had ever heard before, and His miracles left them in awe.

But the ultimate proof of His identity came through His death and resurrection. Jesus was crucified for our sins, buried, and risen on the third day, just as the Scriptures had foretold. He established a new covenant, a new way of relating to God, and He brought redemption and forgiveness to all who would receive Him.

The evidence Is clear: Jesus is the Messiah, the Lamb of God who takes away the sin of the world. He is the King of kings and Lord of lords, the one who brings peace, justice, and righteousness. The prophecies and fulfillments are clear: Jesus is the one who has come to save us from sin.

Beloved, we established that all have sinned and fallen short of God's glory and that sin separates us from God and leads to death. We explored the sacrificial system and the need for a Messiah to redeem us from sin. We confirmed that Jesus is the long-awaited Messiah, the Lamb of God who takes away the sin of the world.

This is a book all about Sin. In order to be complete, we must also study what Jesus, the Messiah, taught about sin.

Jesus' first teaching on sin is found in *Matthew 5:21-22*, where He says:

"You have heard that it was said to those of old, 'You shall not murder, and whoever murders will be liable to judgment.' But I say to you that everyone who is angry with his brother will be liable to judgment; whoever insults his brother will be liable to the council; and whoever says, 'You fool!' will be liable to the hell of fire.'"

Here, Jesus expands the understanding of sin beyond just physical actions to include attitudes and thoughts. He teaches that sin begins in the heart and that we are accountable to God for our inner motivations and intentions.

This teaching challenged the current understanding of sin, which focused primarily on outward actions and adherence to religious rules and regulations. Jesus' teaching on sin highlighted the need for inner purity and a transformed heart and emphasized the importance of love, humility, and mercy.

As He continued to teach, Jesus reinforced this message, saying, "For from within, out of the heart of man, come evil thoughts, sexual immorality, theft, murder, adultery, coveting, wickedness, deceit, sensuality, envy, slander, pride, and foolishness." *(Mark 7:21-22, ESV)*

By teaching that sin originates in the heart, Jesus revealed that true transformation requires a deep, inner work of the Holy Spirit rather than mere external conformity to rules and regulations.

As Jesus began His public ministry, He proclaimed, "The time is fulfilled, and the kingdom of God is at hand; repent and believe in the gospel." *(Mark 1:15, ESV)*

Jesus taught us that acknowledging and confessing our sins is a crucial step in the process of salvation. In Romans 10:9, He says, "If you confess with your mouth that Jesus is Lord and believe in your heart that God raised him from the dead, you will be saved."

This verse is often misunderstood as solely a declaration of faith, but it's also a call to confess our sins and our need for a Savior. The word "confess" (Homologeo in Greek) means to agree with or acknowledge something. In this context, it means acknowledging our sin and our need for Jesus as the sacrificial Lamb of God.

Confessing our sin is not just a one-time event but a lifelong process. It's a recognition that we are sinners in need of God's grace and mercy. When we confess our sins, we agree with God's assessment of our condition and His solution for it.

Jesus' teaching on confession is rooted in the Old Testament concept of confession, where the Israelites would confess their sins to God and to one another *(Leviticus 5:5, Numbers 5:7)*. This confession was a necessary step in the process of restoration and forgiveness.

In the New Testament, Jesus takes this concept further, teaching that confession is not just about acknowledging our sin but also about acknowledging His Lordship and His work on the cross. When we confess Jesus as Lord, we are acknowledging His authority over our lives and His power to save us from sin.

In essence, confession is a posture of humility, recognition, and surrender. It's a recognition that we need Jesus and a surrender to His Lordship and grace. As the apostle John wrote, "If we confess our sins, he is faithful and just to forgive us our sins and to cleanse us from all unrighteousness" *(1 John 1:9, ESV)*.

Jesus' teachings on sin are clear: it's a serious issue that separates us from God and leads to death. He reveals that sin begins in the heart, and we're accountable to God for our inner motivations and intentions.

When confronted with Jesus' profound teachings, people were struck by the weight of their own sinfulness. His words pierced their hearts, revealing the depth of their rebellion against God. This conviction ignited a spark within them, prompting a heartfelt response of repentance and faith.

Consider the Samaritan woman, who, after encountering Jesus, abandoned her mundane task of gathering water and eagerly shared the news of His presence with her entire village. Her transformation was instantaneous, as she surrendered her old life and embraced a new purpose.

Zacchaeus, the tax collector, exemplified a similar transformation. Overwhelmed by Jesus' mercy, he renounced his corrupt practices and pledged to give generously to the poor, demonstrating a radical change of heart.

The disciples, too, were forever changed when they met Jesus. They willingly left behind their familiar lives as fishermen, entrusting themselves to follow Him and discover a new path.

These individuals, like us, were once lost in their own sin and self-centeredness. Yet, upon encountering Jesus, they recognized their need for redemption and surrendered to His loving guidance. Their stories serve as a testament to the power of Jesus' teachings, which continue to awaken hearts today, revealing our own need for forgiveness and prompting us to turn to Him in repentance and faith. Will you respond similarly, acknowledging your own sin and embracing Jesus' offer of redemption?

The stark reality of our individual condition is one of separation from God, not merely because of Adam's ancient transgression but because of our own personal choices. We have each contributed to the chasm between ourselves and our Creator through our thoughts, words, and actions. Our sins, though varied and unique, share a common outcome: death. We have willfully chosen to disobey God's commands, embracing rebellion and rejecting His love.

As a result, we stand condemned, our own guilt and shame isolating us from the One who longs to redeem us. Our desperate need for redemption cries out for a solution, a sacrifice that can atone for our individual sins and bridge the gap between us and God. In this darkest of moments, the promise of the sacrificial Lamb of God shines like a beacon, offering hope and forgiveness to those who recognize their own hopeless condition and cry out for salvation.

Now, it's our turn. Will we respond to Jesus' teachings on sin with conviction and repentance, or will we ignore His words and continue in our sin? The choice is ours. We can continue living under the dominion of the kingdom of sin, or we can break into the Kingdom of God and experience the transformative power of Jesus.

Before we decide, we should understand how Jesus paid for our sins.

"The cross is the central event of human history, and Jesus' sacrifice is the core of our salvation. As Charles Spurgeon said, 'The cross is the pivot of the gospel; the cross is the axis of the world's hope.' On the cross, Jesus bore the weight of our sin, enduring unimaginable physical and spiritual suffering. In agony, He cried out to God yet still extended forgiveness to those who crucified Him.

Jesus' sacrifice paid the debt of sin in full, securing victory over death, sin, and Satan. With His final breath, He proclaimed, 'It is finished,' signifying the completion of His redemptive work.

THE SIN DECEPTION

While Jesus' sacrifice paid the debt of sin in full, securing victory over death, sin, and Satan, it's crucial to recognize that this triumph only becomes personally relevant when we individually accept and appropriate His work on the cross. We must acknowledge that Jesus willingly bore the weight of our sin, taking upon Himself the punishment we deserved and that His sacrifice was made specifically for us.

As we embrace this truth, we can begin to apply Jesus' death to our sins, allowing His finished work to liberate us from the grip of guilt, shame, and condemnation. By faith, we receive the gift of salvation, and His victory becomes our own, freeing us to live in the light of His love, forgiveness, and redemption. As we personalize the cross, we can echo Jesus' triumphant declaration, "It is finished," knowing that our debt has been paid, and we are forever changed.

Take a moment to reflect on your heart. Let the Holy Spirit bring to mind the sins that have separated you from God. Consider the weight of these transgressions and the harm caused to yourself and others. Recognize the devastating truth: the cost of your sin is spiritual death.

As you confront your sin, remember that refusing Jesus' sacrifice leaves you to face the consequences alone. Your debt to God's justice remains unpaid, vulnerable to eternal separation. Every attempt to atone falls short, trapping you in guilt and shame.

Instead, accept Jesus' gift. His substitutionary death settles your debt, adopting you into God's family. His sacrifice frees you from sin's grip, transforming your life to reflect God's love and mercy.

Will you acknowledge your sin and accept redemption?

The redemptive work of Jesus Christ is the very essence of the gospel, a saving work that reconciles humanity to God. On the cross, Jesus bore the punishment for our sins, making amends for our rebellion against God and offering forgiveness that restores our relationship with Him.

Through His sacrifice, Jesus reconciled us to God, bringing us back to a right relationship with our Creator. God declares us righteous, or just, through faith in Jesus' redemptive work, and the Holy Spirit brings new life, transforming us into new creations in Christ.

This transformative work of redemption also brings adoption, where God welcomes us as His beloved children, giving us a new identity and inheritance. As ***Ephesians 1:7*** says, "In Him we have redemption through His blood, the forgiveness of sins, according to the riches of His grace."

Now you know why I keep referring to you as beloved.

Jesus' redemptive work is the power of God for our salvation, a gift of love and grace that we can receive by faith. Will you put your trust in Him and experience the transformative power of His redemption?

As Spurgeon said, 'The cross is the symbol of the love of God, and the seal of the grace of God.' The cross is a beacon of hope in a broken world, revealing God's character – loving, just, and merciful. The cross compels us to respond, to surrender to Jesus' lordship, and to embrace His gift of salvation. Will you behold the cross and let Its power transform your life?"

Let me illustrate what Jesus went through on the cross to pay for your sins.

In the Garden of Gethsemane, Jesus prayed with anguish and sweat, His humanity trembling before the weight of the cost He was about to pay. As He prayed, "Father, if you are willing, take this cup from me; yet not my will, but yours be done" *(Luke 22:42, ESV),* He knew that His journey to the cross was the only way to pay the debt of sin.

Here, we see Jesus' humanity on full display. He is fully God, yet fully man and His struggle in the garden is a testament to the weight of the cross.

Betrayed by Judas' kiss, Jesus was arrested and tried, facing mockery, scorn, and brutality. The Roman soldiers weaved a crown of thorns, piercing His brow, and scourged His back, leaving bloody stripes that cried out for mercy. As the Scriptures say, "Then he released for them Barabbas, and having scourged Jesus, delivered him to be crucified" *(Matthew 27:26, ESV).*

The betrayal and trial of Jesus are a stark reminder of the evil that humanity is capable of.

Imagine Jesus on trial, the only ever sinless one, on trial.

To be sinless means to be without sin, to be perfect and holy. Beloved, Jesus lived a life completely free from sin, never committing a sin or having a sinful thought. He was perfect and blameless, and His character was entirely pure.

As we discussed earlier, sin is a noun that refers to anything that falls short of God's perfect standard. It includes not only actions but also thoughts, attitudes, and motivations that are contrary to God's will.

Now, here's the amazing part: Jesus, who was sinless, was made to become sin for us. This is a profound and mysterious truth that is at the heart of the Christian faith.

As the Bible says, "He made Him who knew no sin to be sin for us, that we might become the righteousness of God in Him" *(2 Corinthians 5:21).*

In other words, Jesus took upon Himself the sin of the world, even though He had none of His own. He became the sacrifice for our sins, bearing the punishment and the shame that we deserved.

By becoming the sacrifice for sin for us, Jesus reconciled us to God, making it possible for us to have a relationship with Him. He took the penalty for our sins upon Himself, and in exchange, He gave us His righteousness.

This is the amazing love and grace of God, and it's a truth that has transformed lives for centuries.

As Jesus carried the cross through the streets of Jerusalem, He walked the Via Dolorosa, a path of sorrow and pain. His mother,

Mary stood at the foot of the cross, her eyes fixed on the tortured face of her son, Jesus. She had watched in horror as they nailed Him to the wood, raising Him up to die. The crowds' jeers and mocking echoed in her ears while Roman soldiers callously cast lots for His clothes.

Despite the unspeakable horror, Mary's heart swelled with pride and wonder. This was her son, the child she nurtured and loved, who brought light and hope to a dark world. As she stood there, a sword of sorrow pierced her heart, recalling Prophet Simeon's words: "A sword will pierce through your own soul also." Now, gazing upon the crucified Christ, Mary knew those words had come true – her soul was pierced, her heart broken.

Yet, amidst pain, she witnessed something greater, something changing history forever. Jesus' hands and feet were pierced by cruel spikes on Golgotha's hill. As He hung on the cross, He cried out, "Father, forgive them, for they know not what they do" (Luke 23:34, ESV). Hours passed in agonizing slow motion toward death. Jesus' pain-wracked body cried out for water, saying, "I thirst" (John 19:28, ESV).

Mary's presence underscored the human cost of the cross – her son's suffering and death, not for His sins, but ours. Our sins caused Mary's anguish and Jesus' crucifixion. Reflect on your own sins, and consider the weight of your transgressions. Recognize the devastating truth: the cost of your sin is spiritual death.

Accepting Jesus' sacrifice settles your debt, adopting you into God's family. His sacrifice frees you from sin's grip, transforming your life to reflect God's love and mercy. Will you acknowledge your sin and accept redemption?

We explored what the crucifixion was like for Mary, but did you ever think about what it was like for God?

Imagine the depth of love required to sacrifice one's own child for the redemption of humanity. On the cross, Jesus bore the weight of our collective sin, every transgression, every rebellion, every thought and deed contrary to God's nature. The burden was crushing, the pain unbearable.

As Jesus hung there, He became sin-personified, absorbing the full force of God's wrath against sin. This act of substitution shielded believers from the devastating consequences of sin, allowing God to remain just while justifying those who trust in Jesus. The cry "My God, my God, why have you forsaken me?" echoes through eternity, a haunting reminder of the temporary separation between Father and Son.

In that moment, God turned away, it's the only time God turned his back on humanity. The full wrath of God on SIN. Unable to gaze upon His Son, tainted by humanity's sin. This anguished decision ensured that God would never forsake those who put their faith in Jesus. The cross demonstrates the magnitude of God's love: He forsook His Son to redeem humanity, guaranteeing that believers will never face eternal separation from Him.

Why did God forsake His Son? So He wouldn't have to forsake you. Beloved, this was all for you.

As Jesus bore the guilt of humanity's sin, He took upon Himself the weight of God's wrath. This sacrifice grants believers forgiveness, righteousness, and reconciliation with God. The cross, once an instrument of shame, became the emblem of redemption, declaring to all: "You are forgiven. You are mine."

Consider the intensity of love that fueled this sacrifice. Jesus' final breath signaled the triumph of love over sin and death. His words, "It is finished," sealed the promise of redemption, assuring humanity that their debt was paid in full.

Through the cross, we glimpse the vast expanse of God's love, a love willing to sacrifice everything for our salvation. This transformative love invites us to surrender to its power, embracing forgiveness, righteousness, and eternal life.

Scriptures remind us: "Greater love has no one than this, that someone lay down his life for his friends" (John 15:13, ESV). "For our sake, he made him to be sin who knew no sin, so that in him we might become the righteousness of God" (2 Corinthians 5:21, ESV).

"For God So Loved the World"

John 3:16 (ESV)

"For God so loved the world, that he gave his only Son, that whoever believes in him should not perish but have eternal life."

This passage from ***John 3:16 is*** one of the most famous verses in the Bible, and it speaks directly to the idea that God sacrificed His only Son for the sake of humanity. Beloved, God did it for you. Jesus willingly went to the cross for you.

In His final moments, Jesus shows us the depth of His love and mercy. Even in the midst of unimaginable pain, He prays for those who have crucified Him. This act of selfless love is a powerful demonstration of God's grace and forgiveness.

As Jesus hangs on the cross, He utters the words: "Father, forgive them, for they do not know what they are doing" *(Luke 23:34).*

This prayer is a stunning example of Jesus' compassion and mercy, and it has been the subject of much commentary and reflection throughout history.

John Calvin, the French theologian, wrote: "Christ, in praying for his enemies, hath given a remarkable proof of his compassion, and hath set us an example, that we may not be provoked by the injuries of men, but may be prepared to forgive and pray for those who wish us evil."

And here's a quote from Matthew Henry, the English Bible commentator, who notes: "This prayer is a wonder, that he should pray for those who had been so cruel to him; and it is a pattern to us, to pray for those who persecute us, and to forgive them from the heart."

In this moment, Jesus shows us that love and forgiveness are not limited by human boundaries or circumstances. His prayer on the cross is a powerful reminder that we are called to love and forgive others, just as God has loved and forgiven us.

Finally, with a loud cry, Jesus declared, "It is finished" *(John 19:30, ESV),* signaling the completion of His redemptive work. At that moment, the curtain of the temple was torn in two, and the earth shook, just as the Scriptures say, "And behold, the curtain of the temple was torn in two, from top to bottom. And the earth shook, and the rocks were split" *(Matthew 27:51, ESV).*

And why did Jesus endure such unimaginable suffering? He did it for you. He took the punishment for your sin, bore the weight of your guilt, and died in your place. The cross was His gift of love, a sacrifice that reconciles you to God. Will you receive this gift and let the power of the cross transform your life?

"The cross is the power of God and the wisdom of God" *(1 Corinthians 1:23-24, ESV)*. It's a symbol of God's love and redemption, where Jesus bore the weight of our sins and reconciled us to Himself.

As Timothy Keller said, "At the cross, God's justice and love are reconciled, and we are reconciled to God." This reconciliation calls us to respond. Jesus said, "If anyone would come after me, let him deny himself and take up his cross and follow me" *(Matthew 16:24, ESV)*.

Taking up our cross means surrendering our will, desires, and dreams to Jesus. It means dying to ourselves and living for Him. Like Paul, we must count everything as loss and regard Christ as our supreme gain *(Philippians 3:8)*.

As Charles Spurgeon comments, "We are not called to bear a cross, but to bear His cross. It is not our own cross, but His cross that we are to take up."

Will you take up His cross and follow Jesus?

What does that mean in practice?

Beloved, Has Jesus captured your heart yet? Do you desperately want a relationship with God? If you do, then the first step is to keep your eyes on God. The second step is to love your neighbor.

That is it...

The final exposing of the lies that bind is to have a relationship with God, you must submit to a religion.

Beloved, the absolute honest truth is that in order to have a relationship with God, you must escape the kingdom of sin and break into the kingdom of God by keeping your eyes fixed on Jesus and your heart fixed on loving His children.

Will you surrender to His Lordship and embrace the transformative power of the cross in your life?

Charles Spurgeon's commentary highlights the significance of the cross as the central event of human history and the pivot of the gospel. IIis words emphasize the depth of God's love and grace and the transformative power of the cross in our lives.

Chapter 18
What Happened When Jesus Died?

fter Jesus died on the cross, His body was pierced by a Roman soldier to confirm His death. Then, He was taken down from the cross and buried in a tomb by Joseph of Arimathea and Nicodemus.

As the apostle Paul wrote, "The wages of sin is death, but the free gift of God is eternal life in Christ Jesus our Lord" *(Romans 6:23, ESV).*

The devastating consequences of sin, which entered the world through Adam's disobedience, continue to ravage humanity, holding dominion over our lives. But the astonishing truth is that Jesus' sacrifice on the cross was not merely a general atonement for the sins of the world but a specific, personal payment for every single one of YOUR sins.

Every lie, every cheat, every theft, every gossip, every hidden thought, and every secret shame was nailed to the cross with Jesus. He bore the weight of your guilt, your shame, and your rebellion, taking upon Himself the punishment you deserve.

Jesus' death was not a vague, collective sacrifice but a precise, individualized act of love. He died for you, specifically for your sins, to save you from the clutches of sin's dominion.

Through His sacrifice, Jesus offers forgiveness, restoration, and reconciliation, inviting you into the right relationship with God. His death was the ultimate expression of love, a love that seeks to free you from the shackles of sin and its devastating consequences.

Will you accept this gift of redemption? Will you acknowledge the depth of your sin and the magnitude of Jesus' sacrifice? Will you surrender your life to Him, allowing His love to transform you and set you free? The choice is yours, but know this: Jesus died for you, and His love awaits your response.

Jesus, fully man and fully God, died on the cross in your place. He was betrayed, mocked, ridiculed, tortured, beaten, lied about, falsely tried, and convicted of crimes He did not commit. Jesus, fully innocent, was put to death in your place. He was killed and buried in the ground for three days.

Yes, beloved, Jesus took the punishment you deserve and died for your sin so you wouldn't have to.

The story doesn't end there.

On the third day, Jesus was raised from the dead, victorious over sin and death. As the angel announced to the women, "He is not here, for he has risen, as he said" *(Matthew 28:6, ESV)*.

The resurrection of Jesus Is a triumphant declaration of His power over sin and death and a guarantee of our own resurrection and eternal life. As Paul wrote, "For if we have been united with him in a death like his, we shall certainly be united with him in a resurrection like his" *(Romans 6:5, ESV)*.

"The death of Christ was the death of sin, and the resurrection of Christ was the resurrection of righteousness."

– John Calvin.

"The cross is the symbol of sin's defeat, and the resurrection is the symbol of sin's destruction."

– Charles Spurgeon

Chapter 19
Conviction

The story of Philip and the Ethiopian eunuch is a powerful example of the conviction and repentance that Jesus teaches about. In this story, we see a man who is searching for truth and is led to Jesus through the witness of Philip.

Acts 8:26-40,

Now, an angel of the Lord said to Philip, "Rise and go toward the south to the road that goes down from Jerusalem to Gaza." This is a desert place. And he rose and went. And there was an Ethiopian, a eunuch, a court official of Candace, queen of the Ethiopians, who was in charge of all her treasure. He had come to Jerusalem to worship and was returning, seated in his chariot, and he was reading the prophet Isaiah. And the Spirit said to Philip, "Go over and join this chariot."

So Philip ran to him and heard him reading Isaiah the prophet and asked, "Do you understand what you are reading?" And he said, "How can I unless someone guides me?" And he invited Philip to come up and sit with him.

And the passage of the Scripture that he was reading was this: "Like a sheep led to the slaughter and like a lamb before its shearer is silent, so he opens not his mouth. In his humiliation, justice was denied him. Who can describe his generation? For his life is taken away from the earth."

And the eunuch said to Philip, "About whom, I ask you, does the prophet say this? About himself or about someone else?" Then Philip opened his mouth, and beginning with this Scripture, he told him the good news about Jesus.

Philip explained how Jesus, the Messiah, had come to earth, lived a sinless life, and died on the cross for the sins of humanity. He shared how Jesus had been buried, but on the third day, He had risen from the dead, defeating sin and death.

Philip shared the good news that through faith in Jesus, we can receive forgiveness for our sins and be reconciled to God. He explained that Jesus is the One who brings light and life to a world in darkness and that He offers living water to all who thirst.

As Philip spoke, the Ethiopian eunuch listened intently, and his heart was opened to the truth. He asked Philip, "What prevents me from being baptized?" And Philip said, "If you believe with all your heart, you may." And he replied, "I believe that Jesus Christ is the Son of God" *(Acts 8:36-37, ESV).*

Beloved, what is preventing you from responding to Jesus like the Ethiopian eunuch did? Is it a lack of understanding, fear, or something else? Whatever it may be, know that Jesus is inviting you to come to Him and find forgiveness and new life.

What you are likely feeling is conviction, the process of becoming aware of our sins and our need for God's grace and mercy. It's a work of the Holy Spirit that leads us to repentance and faith in

Jesus Christ. When we are convicted of our sin, we are faced with a choice: to ignore the conviction and continue in our sin or to respond with repentance and faith.

Jesus didn't just teach about sin; He also provided the solution to our problem with sin, namely death.

Jesus said, "I came not to call the righteous, but sinners." *(Mark 2:17, ESV)* And, "Those who are well have no need of a physician, but those who are sick. I came not to call the righteous, but sinners to repentance." *(Luke 5:31-32, ESV)*

Through His death and resurrection, Jesus provided the ultimate sacrifice for sin, reconciling us to God. As He said, "It is finished." *(John 19:30, ESV)*

Sin is too important to misunderstand. It affects every aspect of human life. As we explored earlier, sin can be both a noun and a verb, representing not only the state of rebellion against God but also the actions that stem from it.

The Bible teaches that sin entered the world through Adam and Eve's disobedience, leading to a fundamental separation from God. Since then, sin has become an inherent part of human nature, manifesting in various ways, such as pride, selfishness, and rebellion.

However, God did not abandon humanity to sin's destructive power. Instead, He initiated a plan of redemption, culminating in the life, death, and resurrection of Jesus Christ.

On the cross, Jesus was pierced for our transgressions, sacrificing Himself for our redemption. He bore the weight of sin, satisfying

God's justice and reconciling us to Himself.

But Jesus' work didn't end there. He was buried, but death couldn't hold Him. He overcame Satan and sin, conquering the kingdom of sin and its ruler. Through His resurrection, Jesus demonstrated His power over death and sin, offering eternal life to all who believe.

As we reflect on these pivotal events, we're reminded of God's boundless love and grace. Jesus' transformative power offers us a new path, one marked by redemption, forgiveness, and reconciliation.

Are you ready to confront your sin and be reconciled to God? If so, I'd like to guide you through the process. Acknowledging our sins, repenting, and accepting Jesus as our sacrificial Lamb is the first step towards redemption.

As the Bible says, "For all have sinned and fall short of the glory of God" *(Romans 3:23).*

Taking personal account of our sins is a crucial step towards freedom and redemption. It requires us to be open and honest with ourselves, acknowledging the thoughts, actions, and attitudes that separate us from God and others. This introspection can be uncomfortable, even painful, but it's essential to confront the depths of our own sinfulness. By doing so, we can begin to see ourselves as God sees us – loved, yet lost; broken, yet beloved. This honest self-assessment allows us to surrender our sins to God, seeking forgiveness and transformation.

As you take this journey of self-reflection, remember that God's light shines not to condemn but to redeem. He desires to expose the darkness of sin in your life, not to shame you, but to free you. Be brave enough to face your sin and humble enough to ask for help.

For in the words of ***Psalm 32:5***, "I acknowledged my sin to you, and I did not cover my iniquity; I said, 'I will confess my transgressions to the Lord,' and you forgave the iniquity of my sin." May God's grace and mercy meet you as you take this courageous step toward honesty and healing.

We must recognize our sinful nature and the separation it creates from God. "For the wages of sin is death, but the gift of God is eternal life in Christ Jesus our Lord."

Who do you say Jesus is? Do you accept Him as your personal Savior, who died on the cross for your sins to reconcile you to God and offer eternal life?

Chapter 20
Confess & Be Saved

If you're ready, it's time to confess with your mouth. As **_Romans 10:9-10_** says, "If you confess with your mouth that Jesus is Lord and believe in your heart that God raised Him from the dead, you will be saved. For with the heart, one believes and is justified, and with the mouth, one confesses and is saved."

Here's a prayer, often called the Sinner's Prayer, to help you express your commitment:

Dear Heavenly Father,

I acknowledge that I am a sinner and have fallen short of Your glory. I repent of my sins and turn to You for forgiveness.

I believe that Jesus Christ is Your Son, who died on the cross for my sins and rose from the dead to give me eternal life.

I invite Jesus into my heart and life, and I receive Him as my Lord and Savior.

Forgive me of my sins, wash me clean, and give me a new heart.

Help me to follow You, obey Your Word, and live according to Your will.

Thank You for saving me, and I surrender my life to Your

guidance and love.

In Jesus' name, I pray.

Amen.

"For God so loved the world, that he gave his only Son, that whoever believes in him should not perish but have eternal life." (John 3:16, ESV)

"If you confess with your mouth that Jesus is Lord and believe in your heart that God raised him from the dead, you will be saved." (Romans 10:9, ESV)

"Everyone who calls on the name of the Lord will be saved." (Romans 10:13, ESV)

Remember, this is just the beginning of your journey. May God bless you as you walk in His grace and truth.

Chapter 21
The Trinity

I probably should have addressed this earlier, but we can't go any further until I explain the Trinity to you.

The Trinity is a fundamental concept in Christianity, describing God as three distinct yet inseparable persons:

1. God the Father: The Creator, Sovereign, and Source of all life. He plans and initiates salvation.

2. Jesus Christ the Son: The Savior, Redeemer, and Mediator. He executes salvation through His life, death, and resurrection.

3. The Holy Spirit: The Helper, Comforter, and Transformer. He applies salvation, guiding believers and empowering them to live for God.

While distinct, the Trinity is one God, sharing the same essence, attributes, and purpose. This unity is demonstrated through their coordinated work in creation, salvation, and the believer's life.

Think of it like a three-stranded cord *(Ecclesiastes 4:12)*: each strand (Father, Son, and Spirit) is unique, yet intertwined and inseparable, forming an unbreakable bond.

The Trinity is a mystery, but understanding its basics helps us appreciate God's complexity, majesty, and love.

After someone accepts Jesus, several things typically follow in the months and years to come.

After accepting Jesus as our Savior, God's Holy Spirit comes to live within us. This is an incredible gift! The Holy Spirit helps us become more like Jesus and live a life that honors God.

In *John 16:5-8*, Jesus is speaking to His disciples about the Holy Spirit's role in the world. He says, "But now I am going to him who sent me, and none of you asks me, 'Where are you going?' But because I have said these things to you, sorrow has filled your heart" *(John 16:5-6, ESV)*.

Jesus knows that His departure will bring sorrow to His disciples, but He reassures them that the Holy Spirit's arrival will bring conviction to the world. He explains, "Nevertheless, I tell you the truth: it is to your advantage that I go away, for if I do not go away, the Helper will not come to you. But if I go, I will send him to you. And when he comes, he will convict the world concerning sin and righteousness and judgment" *(John 16:7-8, ESV)*.

In this passage, Jesus is telling His disciples that the Holy Spirit will convict the world of three things: sin, righteousness, and judgment.

Beloved, did you catch that? The Holy Spirit will convict the world of sin. It's not the job of the church. The church takes the power of conviction from anyone willing to surrender to the kingdom of sin. The church will tell you what sin is, and the church will convict you of its definition of sin if you let it. If not the church, the world will be glad to tell you what right and wrong is. Guilt and shame are always looking for a willing host.

The kingdom of sin only cares that you don't listen to the Holy Spirit.

Beloved, do you want to know what sin is, what it really is?

It's taking your eyes off of God and giving your heart to the kingdom of sin.

The Holy Spirit's conviction is not about making people feel guilty or condemned but about pointing them to Jesus, the only solution for sin. He awakens hearts to receive Jesus as Savior and Lord, leading to repentance, faith, and new life.

The Holy Spirit's conviction is often misunderstood. It's not about making us feel guilty, shameful, or condemned. In fact, the Bible says, "There is therefore now no condemnation for those who are in Christ Jesus" *(Romans 8:1, ESV)*. Conviction is about gently showing us where we've gone wrong and guiding us back to God's path.

Jesus said, "My sheep hear my voice, and I know them, and they follow me" *(John 10:27, ESV)*. The Holy Spirit speaks to us in a voice of love, not condemnation. He reminds us of our identity as beloved children of God, not worthless sinners.

In contrast, the kingdom of sin speaks lies, death, and destruction. It's the voice of shame, guilt, and judgment. If you feel like you're not good enough, that you're a failure, or that God is angry with you, that's not the Holy Spirit. That's the voice of the enemy, trying to steal your identity and purpose.

The Holy Spirit, on the other hand, brings life, freedom, and peace. He teaches us the truth, comforts us in hard times, and guides us into God's plan for our lives. As we listen to His voice, we become more like Jesus, living with purpose, love, and joy.

Remember, the Holy Spirit's voice is one of love, not condemnation. If you're feeling guilty, shameful, or judged, that's not Him. Instead, ask Him to speak truth and love into your heart and listen for His gentle guidance.

Chapter 22
Sanctification

Sanctification is more than just a theological concept – it's a life-changing journey that sets believers apart for God's purposes. Through the Holy Spirit's work, you can experience a profound transformation that makes you holy and pleasing to God.

As you embark on this journey, you'll encounter conviction of sin, leading to genuine repentance. This marks the beginning of a transformed mind, renewed through the Word of God. The Holy Spirit empowers you for obedience, living according to God's will, and enables you to die to self, living for Christ.

This process is lifelong, but its benefits are immeasurable. You'll break free from destructive habits and thought patterns, developing a deeper, more intimate relationship with God. You'll experience joy and peace that transcends circumstances, becoming a powerful witness for Christ and reflecting His character.

Don't settle for a mediocre faith. Embrace the transformative power of sanctification and experience the abundant life Christ promised. Let go of the old and embrace the new, living a life that honors God and reflects the beauty of His holiness.

As we accept Jesus, our journey of sanctification begins, marking a transformative path of growth, not perfection. The Holy Spirit guides and empowers us every step of the way. This journey varies for each individual; some experience radical transformation, like Nicky Cruz, who went from gang leader to evangelist, while others undergo gradual growth, like C.S. Lewis.

Sanctification is a process with ups and downs, resulting in a life honoring God and reflecting Christ's character. It's essential to understand that spiritual growth is a marathon, not a sprint. God's timing is perfect, even when progress seems slow (Isaiah 55:8). Surrendering to His work in our lives fosters patience and trust.

This spiritual rebirth regenerates the human spirit, once dead in sin, now made alive in Christ (Ephesians 2:1-5). Renowned theologian Charles Spurgeon aptly calls regeneration "the greatest of all miracles." Inner transformation is a deep and lasting renovation of the heart, mind and spirit, powered by the Holy Spirit.

The Holy Spirit convicts us of sin, guides us into truth and empowers us to live anew (John 16:8-15). He brings conviction, illuminates God's Word and grants strength to overcome sin. As we yield to the Holy Spirit, we experience a new desire to please God, a new love for others and a new sense of purpose.

Again, Don't be discouraged by slow progress; God's timing is perfect. Surrender to His work, and you'll become more like Jesus. Surrender what you can. If the Holy Spirit is telling you to give up anger, start there. If He is telling you to go feed the neighbor, start there.

As 2 Corinthians 5:17 states, "If anyone is in Christ, the new creation has come: The old has gone, the new is here!" Embark on this transformative journey, discovering the depths of God's love and grace.

Before we go on, I want to address another common misconception about sin.

Oftentimes, I see people struggling with "being good enough for church." I hear people say, "When I quit smoking, or after I stop drinking, I will go to church."

First, that is religion talking, not relationship, and second, that is not how it works.

As we journey through life, we're faced with a choice: to remain in the kingdom of sin or to break into the Kingdom of God. The kingdom of sin, with its lies and deceit, seeks to keep us in bondage, whispering that we're not enough and that we'll never be free. But Jesus has already shattered those chains, freeing us from sin's dominion through His sacrifice and victory.

Chapter 23

Breaking Into The Kingdom Of God

Now, it's our task to break into the Kingdom of God, to actively seek and experience the fullness of God's presence, power, and joy. This requires effort, dedication, and a willingness to surrender to God's will. We must strive to enter the Kingdom, pressing into its transformative power and seeking to conform to the image of Christ.

But what does this look like in our daily lives? It means recognizing the subtle influences of sin and actively choosing to overcome them. It means seeking God's truth and wisdom rather than relying on our own understanding. It means embracing the freedom Jesus offers rather than returning to the bondage of sin.

Here we have another opportunity to Expose the Lies that Bind: Overcoming Sin is Not Enough.

For far too long, we've been misled by a partial truth: that overcoming sin is solely about escaping or avoiding it. However, this perspective only scratches the surface. The reality is more profound. To truly triumph over sin, we must also break into the kingdom of God.

Sin is not just an individual action but a dominant force that reigns within us. It's a kingdom that enslaves, manipulating our thoughts, emotions and actions. Escaping sin doesn't merely mean fleeing its consequences, but breaking out of the kingdom of sin requires confronting and dismantling its strongholds.

Our approach must shift from mere escape artists to kingdom invaders. We must boldly enter the realms where sin holds sway, confronting the lies, fears and doubts that empower it. This invasion demands courage, perseverance and the power of the Holy Spirit. Jesus didn't just escape sin; He invaded the kingdom of darkness, conquering its depths.

Through Jesus' victory, we're empowered to do the same. By embracing our identity in Christ, we become agents of God's kingdom, equipped to overthrow sin's reign and establish God's rule within us. We identify and challenge the lies that fuel sin, confront fears, renounce doubts and replace sin's influence with God's truth.

In Christ, we're not just overcomers but we are also conquerors. We don't merely escape the kingdom of sin; and we actively work against it. We establish God's reign within us. This victory transforms us, empowering us to live under God's kingdom rule.

As Jesus said, "The kingdom of God is not coming with signs to be observed, nor will they say, 'Look, here it is!' or 'There!' for behold, the kingdom of God is in the midst of you" *(Luke 17:20-21, ESV)*.

Think of it this way: breaking addiction is less about escaping the grip of substance abuse and more about ending the separation and isolation from God. It's not just about stopping a behavior but about starting a new life. It's not just about escaping darkness but about embracing light.

As Paul wrote, "For the kingdom of God is not a matter of eating and drinking but of righteousness and peace and joy in the Holy Spirit" *(Romans 14:17, ESV).*

We've been so focused on escaping the kingdom of sin that we've forgotten the thrill of pursuing the Kingdom of God. We've settled for behavior modification when we could be experiencing kingdom transformation. We've been content with 12-step programs when we could be living out the Sermon on the Mount.

As Jesus taught, "Seek first the kingdom of God and his righteousness, and all these things will be added to you" *(Matthew 6:33, ESV).*

It's time for a new approach. It's time to shift our focus from breaking out to breaking in. It's time to stop just escaping sin and start chasing Jesus. It's time to experience the abundant life He offers, to live out the Kingdom of God in our daily lives, and to transform our neighborhoods with His love and presence.

- Luke 16:16 - "The Law and the Prophets were until John; since then, the good news of the kingdom of God is preached, and everyone forces his way into it."

- Romans 6:6-7 - "We know that our old self was crucified with him in order that the body of sin might be brought to nothing so that we would no longer be enslaved to sin. For one who has died has been set free from sin."

- Galatians 5:1 - "For freedom, Christ has set us free; stand firm therefore, and do not submit again to a yoke of slavery."

- John 10:10 - "The thief comes only to steal and kill and destroy. I came that they may have life and have it abundantly."

Chapter 24
Baptism

As you step into your new life in Christ, you may feel the same draw that the Ethiopian eunuch had. To be baptized. It is a very important step in the right direction for a new believer. Before you make the decision, you should understand Baptism from a Biblical perspective.

The two types of baptisms are:

1. Water Baptism (symbolic): A public declaration of faith, symbolizing our old life being washed away and our new life in Christ (***Romans 6:3-4, ESV***: "Do you not know that all of us who have been baptized into Christ Jesus were baptized into his death? We were buried therefore with him by baptism into death, in order that, just as Christ was raised from the dead by the glory of the Father, we too might walk in newness of life.")

2. Baptism of the Holy Spirit (spiritual): A divine encounter where the Holy Spirit comes upon us, empowering us for service and witness (***Acts 1:4-5, 8***, ESV: "And while staying with them he ordered them not to depart from Jerusalem, but to wait for the promise of the Father…for John baptized with water, but you will be baptized with the Holy Spirit not many days from now…But you will receive power when the Holy Spirit has come upon you,

and you will be my witnesses in Jerusalem and in all Judea and Samaria, and to the end of the earth.")

When we put our faith in Jesus, every believer is instantly made clean and becomes a dwelling place for the Holy Spirit (*1 Corinthians 6:19-20, ESV*: "Or do you not know that your body is a temple of the Holy Spirit within you, whom you have from God? You are not your own, for you were bought with a price. So glorify God in your body.")

The Father is in Heaven, Jesus is at His right side, but the Holy Spirit resides in us and all around us (*John 14:16-17, ESV*: "And I will ask the Father, and he will give you another Helper, to be with you forever…He dwells with you and will be in you").

The Baptism of the Holy Spirit is not a separate experience from salvation. With salvation comes the indwelling of the Holy Spirit. The indwelling of the Spirit is not the end of the Holy Spirit. Christians can expect to experience the active Spirit of God being used in them and through them to bless others.

The Holy Spirit comes upon us, empowering us for service and witness (*Acts 2:1-4, ESV*: "When the day of Pentecost arrived, they were all together in one place…And they were all filled with the Holy Spirit and began to speak in other tongues as the Spirit gave them utterance").

As the renowned theologian Charles Spurgeon once said: "The baptism of the Holy Spirit is not a mere sentiment, but a mighty fact. It is not a fancy but a reality. It is not a myth, but a glorious truth, which has been experienced by thousands of believers."

Now, let's return to your Baptism in water.

This very special act is a public declaration of your faith, a powerful symbol of your old life being washed away and your new life in Christ. Through baptism, you're boldly telling the world: "I'm a follower of Jesus, and I'm committed to living for Him."

As the renowned evangelist Billy Graham once said, "Baptism is a symbolic act, but it's an act that speaks volumes about our commitment to Christ." By choosing baptism, you're following in the footsteps of countless believers throughout history who have declared their faith publicly.

Q: Do I have to be fully immersed in water, or will sprinkling work?

A: "Go therefore and make disciples of all nations, baptizing them in the name of the Father and of the Son and of the Holy Spirit" (*Matthew 28:19*). While the mode of baptism is not specified, the act of baptism is a symbol of our old life being washed away and our new life in Christ. Either immersion or sprinkling can be pleasing to God, as it's an act of the heart, not of duty. (Commentary: The focus is on the heart's commitment, not the mode of baptism.)

Q: Do I have to wait until I am a certain age to be baptized?

A: "Whoever believes and is baptized will be saved, but whoever does not believe will be condemned" (*Mark 16:16*). While there is no set age when you choose to be baptized, you are making a public declaration of your commitment to Jesus Christ and His Kingdom. If you can genuinely believe in your heart and confess with your mouth to be saved, no one should stop you. (Commentary: Age is not a barrier to baptism, but genuine faith is essential.)

Q: Do I have to say something special or recite a specific set of words at my baptism?

A: "If you confess with your mouth that Jesus is Lord and believe in your heart that God raised him from the dead, you will be saved" (***Romans 10:9***). No, this is an act of love, not some rule or ritual. This is about exposing yourself as a new creation, a member of the body of Christ, a living testimony to His goodness. (Commentary: Baptism is a public declaration, not a recitation of specific words.)

Q: Can I be baptized multiple times?

A: "For as many of you as were baptized into Christ have put on Christ" (***Galatians 3:27***). The public profession of your faith should be part of your daily life. If you have been baptized into the Kingdom of God by your relationship with Jesus, there is no need to rebaptize. However, if your original baptism lacked understanding or genuine commitment, it would bless you to be baptized again as you rededicate your life to Jesus. (Commentary: Baptism is a one-time act, but our walk with God is lifelong.)

Q: What about babies? Can you baptize babies? While infant baptism is not explicitly mentioned in Scripture, dedicating a child to the Lord is a beautiful way to seek His blessing and guidance from an early age.

In the Kingdom of God, children are precious and loved, and Jesus said, "Let the little children come to me and do not hinder them, for to such belongs the kingdom of heaven. Truly, I say to you, whoever does not receive the kingdom of God like a child shall not enter it." (***Matthew 19:14***)

Jesus' words highlight the value and innocence of children, and their natural trust and faith are an example to us all. Whether baptized as infants or dedicating their lives to Jesus at an older age, children are precious in His sight and beloved members of the Kingdom of God.

In fact, *Matthew 18:10* says, "See that you do not despise one of these little ones. For I tell you that in heaven their angels always see the face of my Father who is in heaven." This verse reminds us of children's special place in God's heart.

Children are a gift from God, and their presence in our lives is a blessing. As we dedicate them to the Lord and seek His guidance, we can trust that He will watch over them and guide them into a deep and abiding relationship with Himself.

Chapter 25
Faith & The Bible

The next thing we should talk about is the wonder of faith! It's the spark that ignites our journey with God, the fuel that sustains us, and the anchor that holds us secure. But where does faith come from, how do we grow it, and what happens when we feel it slipping away?

The Bible tells us that faith comes from hearing the message of God's Word (***Romans 10:17***). It's the response of our hearts to the truth of who God is and what He has done for us. And as we hear and respond to His Word, our faith grows.

We should talk about getting a Bible if you don't have one.

The Bible is a collection of sacred writings revered by Christians as the inspired word of God. It's a library of 66 books written by various authors over centuries, yet remarkably cohesive in its message.

The Bible contains:

- Old Testament (39 books): Creation, history, poetry, prophecy, and wisdom literature
- New Testament (27 books): Life, teachings, death, and resurrection of Jesus Christ, plus early church history and

letters

Modern translations are great because they:

- Use original languages (Hebrew, Greek, Aramaic) for accuracy
- Update archaic language for clarity
- Provide fresh perspectives without altering meaning

I recommend the English Standard Version (ESV) for its:

- Balance between accuracy and readability
- Literary style, making it enjoyable to read
- Faithfulness to original texts

The ESV is a reliable choice for personal study, teaching, and worship. Other great translations include NASB, NIV, and NKJV. Ultimately, choose a translation that resonates with you and fosters a deeper connection with God's word. Now back to faith as a gift of God.

But how do we nurture this precious gift? The apostle Paul encourages us to "seek the Lord and His strength; seek His face continually" (*1 Chronicles 16:11*). We grow our faith by seeking God, His presence, and His power in our lives.

Yet, there may be times when our faith wavers. We may feel like we're losing our grip on God. What do we do then? The writer of Hebrews reminds us to "hold fast the confession of our hope without wavering, for He who promised is faithful" (*Hebrews 10:23*). We cling to the promises of God, we cry out to Him in our darkness, and we trust in His faithfulness.

Beloved, faith is not about our own strength or abilities but about the power and grace of God. As Paul says, "I am not ashamed of the gospel, for it is the power of God for salvation to everyone who believes" (***Romans 1:16***). We should embrace this gift of faith, nurture it, and trust in the God who is always faithful.

Chapter 26
Fellowship Of Believers

Fellowship with believers is the lifeblood of our spiritual journey. When we connect with a local church or Christian community, we experience the power of togetherness and the joy of shared purpose.

As the apostle John wrote, "And by this we know that we have come to know Him if we keep His commandments. He who says, 'I have come to know Him,' and does not keep His commandments, is a liar, and the truth is not in him; but whoever keeps His word, in him the love of God has truly been perfected. By this we know that we are in Him" (*1 John 2:3-5*).

In fellowship, we find support, encouragement, and spiritual growth. We learn from one another, pray for each other, and together, we serve the world around us. As *Hebrews 10:24-25* says, "And let us consider how we may spur one another on toward love and good deeds, not giving up meeting together, as some are in the habit of doing, but encouraging one another—and all the more as you see the Day approaching."

Fellowship is not just a nice-to-have. It's a must-have for every believer. It's where we experience the body of Christ in action, where we use our gifts and talents to serve one another, and where we grow in our love for God and for each other.

Christians need Christians because we are not meant to walk alone. We need the support, encouragement, and accountability that comes from being part of a community of believers. We need to be reminded of the truth, to be challenged in our faith, and to be loved and accepted for who we are.

A Bible-believing church is a community that holds fast to the Word of God, proclaims the Gospel of Jesus Christ, and lives out its faith in practical and tangible ways. It's a place where believers gather to worship, to learn, and to serve together. It's a place where we can be real, where we can be vulnerable, and where we can be transformed by the power of God's love.

"The local church is not just a building or a denomination, but a community of broken people, redeemed by the grace of God, and empowered by the Holy Spirit to love and serve the world around them. It's a place where the messy and the broken, the sinner and the saint, can come together to experience the power of the Gospel and to be transformed by the love of Jesus Christ."

— Matt Chandler, lead pastor of The Village Church

This quote captures the essence of what the local church should be – a community of imperfect people united by their love for God and their desire to serve others.

Chapter 27
Discipleship

Discipleship is the pathway to spiritual growth and maturity. When we commit to following Jesus, we're not just starting a new journey; we're becoming part of a long line of disciples who have walked this path before us. As Jesus said, "If anyone would come after me, let him deny himself and take up his cross and follow me" (*Matthew 16:24*).

Through discipleship programs or mentoring, we can deepen our understanding of God's Word, develop a stronger prayer life, and learn to apply biblical principles to our everyday lives. We're not just learning from others; we're also learning to obey Jesus' command to make disciples of all nations (*Matthew 28:19*).

Discipleship is not just about knowledge; it's about transformation. It's about becoming more like Jesus and living a life that honors Him. As Paul wrote, "My dear children, for whom I am again in the pains of childbirth until Christ is formed in you" (*Galatians 4:19*).

Discipleship is a lifelong journey, and it's not always easy. But with the guidance of the Holy Spirit, the support of a community, and a willingness to learn and grow, we can become the disciples Jesus is calling us to be.

A Bible-believing church prioritizes discipleship because it knows that spiritual growth and maturity are essential for every believer. It's not just about attending services or programs; it's about becoming a fully devoted follower of Jesus Christ.

As we grow in our faith, we can't help but overflow with the love and grace of God. We're compelled to share the Gospel with others, to spread the good news of salvation and redemption. This isn't just a duty, but a privilege – to tell others about the transformative power of Jesus Christ in our lives.

The apostle Peter wrote, "But in your hearts honor Christ the Lord as holy, always being prepared to make a defense to anyone who asks you for a reason for the hope that is in you" (*1 Peter 3:15*). We're called to be ready to share our story, to give a reason for the hope that we have.

Sharing our faith isn't about forcing others to believe but about freely offering the gift of grace we've received. It's about loving others enough to tell them the truth and trusting God with the results.

As we share our faith, we're not just changing lives; we're also growing in our own faith. We're deepening our understanding of God's Word and developing the boldness and confidence that comes from knowing Him.

A Bible-believing church encourages its members to share their faith, knowing that this is the natural overflow of a life transformed by Jesus Christ. We're not just called to be disciples; we're called to make disciples – to go and tell, to share and spread the love and redemption of our Savior.

As we walk with God, our lives begin to transform in profound ways. We start to exhibit the fruit of the Spirit, characteristics that are hallmarks of a life fully surrendered to Him. Paul writes in *Galatians 5:22-23*, "But the fruit of the Spirit is love, joy, peace, patience, kindness, goodness, faithfulness, gentleness, self-control; against such things there is no law."

Chapter 28
The Fruit Of The Spirit.

This fruit is not something we can manufacture or produce on our own. It's the natural byproduct of a life lived in harmony with God. As we abide in Him, we begin to experience the transformative power of His presence.

Love becomes our default, joy our constant companion, and peace our steady anchor. Patience, kindness, and goodness become our guiding principles. Faithfulness, gentleness, and self-control become our marks of character.

The fruit of the Spirit is not just a list of virtues but a manifestation of God's character in us. It's the evidence of a life fully surrendered to Him, a life that is being transformed from the inside out.

As we walk with God, we exhibit this fruit in abundance so that the world may see and know the love and grace of our Savior.

As we grow in our faith, we begin to discover and develop spiritual gifts that enable us to build up the body of Christ. The apostle Paul writes, "To each is given the manifestation of the Spirit for the common good" (*1 Corinthians 12:7*).

These gifts are not just talents or skills but supernatural

empowerments that allow us to serve others and glorify God. Whether it's evangelism, teaching, service, or other gifts, we are called to use them to bless others and edify the church.

As we discover and develop our spiritual gifts, we experience a sense of purpose and fulfillment. We're no longer just spectators but active participants in the mission of God. We're able to make a real difference in the lives of others and to see the kingdom of God advance.

The Bible encourages us to "earnestly desire the spiritual gifts" (*1 Corinthians 14:1*) and to "use them to serve one another, as good stewards of God's varied grace" (*1 Peter 4:10*). May we embrace our spiritual gifts and use them to build up the body of Christ, that the world may see and know the love and power of our Savior.

A Bible-believing church encourages its members to discover, develop, and use their spiritual gifts, knowing that this is essential for the growth and health of the church. By using our gifts to serve others, we experience the joy and fulfillment that comes from being part of the body of Christ.

As believers, we are not merely saved from our sins, but we are also being transformed by God's grace. Ongoing sanctification is the process by which we grow in holiness, becoming more like Jesus every day. The apostle Paul wrote, "And we all, with unveiled face, beholding the glory of the Lord, are being transformed into the same image from one degree of glory to another" (*2 Corinthians 3:18*).

Sanctification is not a one-time event but a lifelong journey. It's the daily surrender of our will to God, the constant renunciation of sin, and the ongoing pursuit of righteousness. As we yield to the Holy Spirit, He works in us, transforming our thoughts, words, and actions.

Ongoing sanctification is not about striving for perfection but about progressing in holiness. It's the recognition that we are working in progress, that God is still molding and shaping us, and that His transformative work in our lives is ongoing.

As we continue to grow in holiness, we become more effective witnesses for Christ, more compassionate servants of others, and more passionate lovers of God. May we embrace this lifelong journey of sanctification, surrendering to God's transforming work in our lives and becoming more like Jesus every day.

Ultimately, the greatest blessing of a Christian life is the assurance of eternal life with God. As Jesus said, "I am the resurrection and the life. Whoever believes in me, though he dies, yet shall he live, and everyone who lives and believes in me shall never die" (*John 11:25-26*). This promise gives us hope and comfort, knowing that our sins are forgiven and that we will spend eternity with our loving Father.

A Christian life is marked by a personal relationship with God, spiritual growth, fellowship with believers, discipleship, sharing their faith, exhibiting the fruit of the Spirit, discovering and developing spiritual gifts, ongoing sanctification, and the assurance of eternal life.

"The Christian life is the most joyful, peaceful, and fulfilling life possible. It is a life of purpose, meaning, and direction. It is a life that is lived to the glory of God, and it is a life that is filled with the blessings of God." - David Jeremiah.

Please note that everyone's journey is unique, and not everyone will follow this exact path. However, these milestones often mark the journey of someone who has accepted Jesus.

Chapter 29
Closing Remarks

In the beginning, God created a perfect world, but sin entered and disrupted His plan. Through the ages, God revealed the complexity of sin, showing its far-reaching effects and our inability to overcome it alone. From the sacrifices of the Old Testament to the ultimate sacrifice of Jesus Christ, God demonstrated His love and desire to reconcile us to Himself.

Sin is both a verb and a noun, an action and a state of being. It's a verb, a choice we make to disobey God's commands and a noun, the orientation of our heart towards self that separates us from God. And we're all guilty of it.

Everyone has sinned, everyone deserves death, and everyone needs a Savior.

Sin has also established a kingdom, a dominion of darkness and rebellion against God. This kingdom is ruled by Satan, the father of lies, who seeks to keep us in bondage to sin and separate us from God's love.

But Jesus is the final sacrifice for our sins, the only one worthy to atone for our transgressions. He took upon Himself the penalty of our sin, dying on the cross to pay the price of our redemption. And through His resurrection, He defeated sin and death, offering us eternal life and reconciliation with God. By His victory, He also defeated the kingdom of sin, establishing His own kingdom of love, forgiveness, and redemption.

We've seen how sin separates us from God, leading to spiritual death and eternal separation. We've explored how sin affects our relationships, causing hurt and pain for ourselves and others. We've examined the nature of sin, understanding it as a heart issue that manifests in our thoughts, words, and actions. But we've also seen the hope of salvation, the promise of forgiveness and transformation through Jesus Christ.

So, what shall we do? Will we continue to be enslaved by sin, or will we turn to Jesus and receive His gift of salvation? Will we allow sin to define us, or will the grace of God transform us? The choice is ours. We can remain in the kingdom of sin, or we can enter the kingdom of God, where love, joy, and peace reign supreme.

Come to Jesus today, and let His love and grace transform your life forever. Acknowledge your sin, confess your need for a Savior, and receive His gift of eternal life. As you begin this new journey, remember to seek guidance in God's Word, wisdom in prayer, and support in fellowship with other believers. May God bless you as you seek Him, and may His love and grace transform your life forever.

References

- Burke, T. (2018). Me Too. In M. B. Smith (Ed.), The Oxford Handbook of Women and Gender in War and Conflict (pp. 1-5). Oxford University Press.
- National Sexual Violence Resource Center. (2020). Sexual Assault Awareness and Prevention.
- The New York Times. (2018). The #MeToo Movement.
- Pew Research Center. (2020). Americans' Views on #MeToo Movement and Sexual Harassment.
- Council of Economic Advisers. (2017). The Economic Costs of the Opioid Crisis.
- Gomes, T., et al. (2018). The Burden of Opioid-Related Mortality. Journal of Addiction Medicine, 12(5), 381-388.
- Koch, A. L., et al. (2019). The Intersection of Opioid Use Disorder and Mental Health. Journal of Clinical Psychology, 75(1), 15-25.
- National Institute on Drug Abuse. (2020). Opioid Overdose Crisis.
- Augustine. (397). Confessions.
- Calvin, J. (1842). Commentary on Genesis.
- Henry, M. (1994). Matthew Henry's Commentary on the Whole Bible.

Sources

American Psychological Association: "The Effects of Pornography on Individuals and Society"

National Institute of Mental Health: "Pornography and Sexual Aggression"

Harvard Health Publishing: "Rethinking Pornography Addiction"

Sources

- "The Effects of Casual Sex on Mental Health" (Psychology Today)

- "Hookup Culture and Mental Health" (The American Psychological Association)

- "Sexual Health and Hookup Culture" (Centers for Disease Control and Prevention)

Sources

- "The Effects of Legalism" (Journal of Biblical Studies)

- "Inner Transformation" (Christianity Today)

- "Historical Context and Biblical Interpretation" (Theological Studies)

Sources

- "Amazing Grace: The Life of John Newton" by Bruce Hindmarsh

- "The Church of England and Slavery" by the Church of England's official website

END